CONTENTS

A NOTE TO PARENTS

The age in which games were considered simple time-wasters is over. These days, games such as Minecraft are nurturing children's creativity while teaching computational thinking. The problem, however, is in transferring and applying these skills. The fact is that most coding tutorials are boring, focusing solely on the theory rather than the infinite number of things you can do with the techniques they teach.

In contrast, *Coding for Minecrafters* aims to turn coding from a chore into a hobby. We'll explore coding concepts such as variables, loops, and functions, but the real emphasis is always on the ways these can be used to create anything your child can imagine.

This book uses Minecraft-themed settings and characters to provide a familiar backdrop for your child's learning. Whether they want to make music with Steve, animate a creeper, or mod the game directly, there's something for everyone inside! Today's novice coders are tomorrow's tech giants, after all, and *Coding for Minecrafters* aims to help your child take their first steps on a long, exciting journey of discovery.

REQUIREMENTS

- A copy of Minecraft for Windows or macOS

- A TextEditor

- For Windows users, Notepad is fine, as is TextEdit for macOS. That said, we recommend using the color-coded interfaces offered by the following programs, if possible:

  For Windows: Notepad++
  Available at: https://notepad-plus-plus.org

  For macOS: Atom
  Available at: https://atom.io

- A web browser and Internet connection. Certain aspects of HTML5 do not function properly in Internet Explorer or Mozilla Firefox, so I recommend using Google Chrome if at all possible. It's important to allow pop-ups on the pages we create by clicking the button at the right-hand side of the address bar.

  Google Chrome is available at: https://www.google.com/chrome/

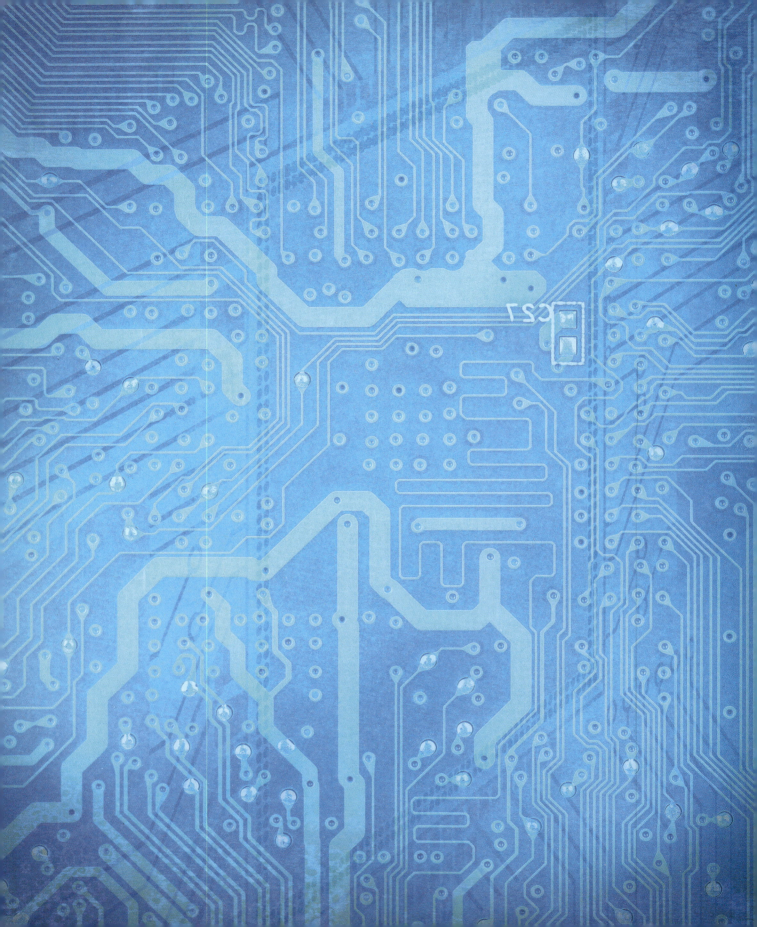

WEB DESIGN

Mission 1
Steve's Sensational Blog: Build a Website

Steve wants to create a blog but doesn't know how. With a simple TextEditor and the right code, we can help him out! We're going to use a coding language called HTML to build the basic parts of Steve's website for him. Once have this solid start, we can add all sorts of fun extras.

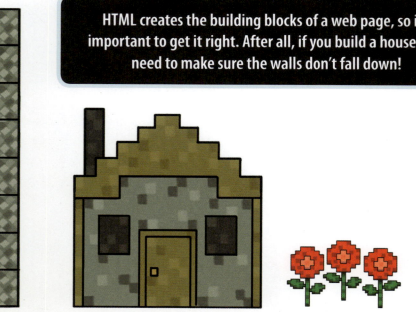

HTML creates the building blocks of a web page, so it's important to get it right. After all, if you build a house, you need to make sure the walls don't fall down!

LET'S GET SET

I. Open up your TextEditor (check back with Requirements on page v, if needed).

The important thing to know is that **HTML ALWAYS STARTS WITH THESE LINES:**

```
<!DOCTYPE html>
<html>
```

The DOCTYPE tells your browser what version of HTML you're using. This line used to be really long, but since HTML5 was released, it's a lot easier to remember. That's good because it has to be written at the top of every HTML page you make! Go ahead and type these lines in now.

2. See the text in the pointy brackets? These are called **TAGS**. There's something else, too. **MOST TAGS NEED TO BE CLOSED** by typing them again, but with a forward slash before the first letter. Here, we've opened our HTML section with <html>. We'll close it again down at the bottom of the page like so:

```
</html>
```

3. Now, like Steve, **HTML PAGES HAVE A HEAD AND A BODY** (no legs, though!). Underneath the <html> tag at the top, type:

The head is where we put important information, and the body is where we put things that we want to show up on the website. So let's add some content!

```
<html>

<head>
</head>

<body>
</body>

</html>
```

4. In the body section, we're going to add a set of <div> tags. **A <DIV> IS JUST A CONTAINER** where we can put other objects. Go ahead and **CREATE TWO <DIV> ELEMENTS** inside your <body> tags. Make sure to close them, too!

CONTAINER MAGIC   X

Think of <div> elements like a chest in Minecraft—created to keep things nice and organized, probably better than your bedroom. Just like a chest can help a room look better, we're going to use <div> tags to improve the look of Steve's website. It's a bit of coding that makes a big difference!

Now click in front of your <div> and **PRESS TAB** (this is next to the Q button on your keyboard). See how the text moved to the right? Coders do this so they can easily see which elements are contained inside others. Since the <div> tags are inside the <body>, they all need to be pushed in a little.

We've also **ADDED AN ID FOR EACH <DIV>.** This isn't important yet, but don't worry! I'll explain what IDs do later. You can change this ID to whatever you want, but make sure you don't add any spaces!

```
<!DOCTYPE html>
<html>

<head>
</head>

<body>

    <div id = 'topbar'>
    </div>

    <div id = 'mainsection'>
    </div>

</body>

</html>
```

READY TO GO!

5. Now that we have our containers ready, let's put something in them!

```
<body>

    <div id = 'topbar'>
        <p> Hi, I'm Steve! Welcome to my website! </p>
    </div>

    <div id = 'mainsection'>
        <p> Who am I?: </p>
        <p> What do I do?: </p>
        <p> My favorite things are: </p>
    </div>

</body>
```

See how we've put <p> tags inside the divs? P stands for paragraph, and these elements let you **ADD TEXT** to your website! They also automatically add a new line at the end to keep everything separated and easy to read.

TRY ANSWERING THE QUESTIONS IN THE <P> TAGS. Just type your answers straight in here, before the "</p>".

6. CLICK FILE in the top-left, then choose **SAVE AS**. Now it's time to give your page a name. Since this will be our website's main page, name it **"INDEX".** You might want to create a folder to keep all of the files you'll create nice and organized.

If there's a menu that says **SAVE AS TYPE** at the bottom, it may give you the option to save as "HTML" or "Hyper Text Markup Language". Do this, if possible. If you can't find these options, save as **ALL FILES** and add ".html" to the end of your file name. When you're ready, click **SAVE**.

File name:	index
Save as type:	Hyper Text Markup Language file (*.html;*.htm;*.shtml;*.shtm;*.xhtml;*.xht;*.hta)

File name:	index.html
Save as type:	All Files

7. Ready to see what we've created? Go to wherever you saved the page and **CLICK OPEN THE HTML FILE**. Let's see what Steve's site looks like!

Hi, I'm Steve! Welcome to my website!

WHO AM I?: I'm a miner!

WHAT DO I DO?: I build things and go on adventures!

MY FAVORITE THINGS ARE: Diamonds and exploring

It looks good, but it's kind of plain, right? Let's add a picture!

8. Open up your favorite drawing program, and **DRAW AND COLOR A PICTURE OF STEVE**. Try to get rid of as much white space as possible; otherwise, your picture will have a big white border on the website. This is called **CROPPING**. Click the squares that appear when you click outside of your image to make the picture as small as possible without cutting off any parts of Steve.

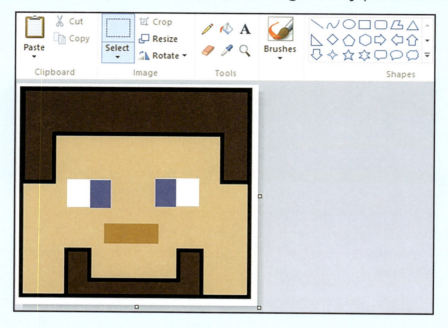

Once you're done, click **SAVE** and name your drawing **STEVE.JPG**. Make sure to save it as a JPEG file in the same folder as your HTML document.

9. Now go back to your TextEditor and in the top <div>, enter the following:

```
<img id ='steve' src='steve.jpg'/>
```

SEE HOW WE GAVE THE PICTURE AN ID? This is in case we want to move it or change its size later. The "src" part tells the website where to find the right image. Unlike most tags, <img> tags can be closed with "/>" instead of "</img>", but you can use whichever way you prefer.

Reload the website, and your picture should appear!

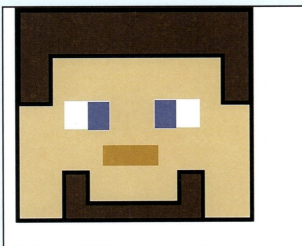

Hi, I'm Steve! Welcome to my website!

WHO AM I?: I'm a miner!

WHAT DO I DO?: I build things and go on adventures!

MY FAVORITE THINGS ARE: Diamonds and exploring

Great work to build your first simple website! We aren't finished yet, though; in the next chapter, we'll explain how to make Steve's site look amazing by adding a splash of color.

MISSION 2
FUN WITH STYLE: LET CSS HELP STEVE

Now that you know the basics of HTML, we're going to add something new called Cascading Style Sheets (CSS, for short). CSS is easy to understand and will help you make your website look just like you want! Ready to discover all you can do for Steve in Mission 2?

Steve can do lots of things. And so can his website, with your help and CSS!

LET'S GET SET

I. Open the "index" HTML file you created for Steve's website in Mission 1. **ADD THE FOLLOWING TEXT** inside your <head> tags at the top of the page:

```
<link rel="stylesheet" type="text/css" href="style.css">
```

This tells our HTML page where to find our CSS file. The "href" section tells it the name of our CSS file. This code says the CSS file is called "style.css", so let's create that now.

2. Open a new file in your TextEditor. Name it **STYLE.CSS** and save it in the same folder as your web page, making sure to change **SAVE AS TYPE** to CSS if there's the option. If not, just add ".css" to the end of the file name.

READY TO GO!

3. CSS WORKS BY APPLYING CERTAIN EFFECTS TO HTML TAGS. We'll start with something simple. In your CSS file, type:

```
p{

color: red;

}
```

Now save the file again (you have to do this after every change) and reload the web page. Your text should now be red!

Hi, I'm Steve! Welcome to my website!

WHO AM I?: I'm a miner!

WHAT DO I DO?: I build things and go on adventures!

MY FAVORITE THINGS ARE: Diamonds and exploring

So how does this all work? **IN CSS, THE PART OUTSIDE THE BRACKETS IS THE TAG WE WANT TO CHANGE.** In this case, I've written "p", to select the <p> tags in our HTML. Inside the brackets, we say what we want to change about these tags. You can try typing different colors in here, instead of red.

4. Why not **CHANGE THE BACKGROUND COLOR,** too? To do this, type:

```
body {

        background-color: blue;

}
```

ADVENTURES WITH HEX   X

If you're really feeling adventurous, try searching Google for "CSS color picker", and using the hex value instead of a color name. The hex value is the series of numbers and letters with a "#" symbol in front. I've circled it in red in the image below.

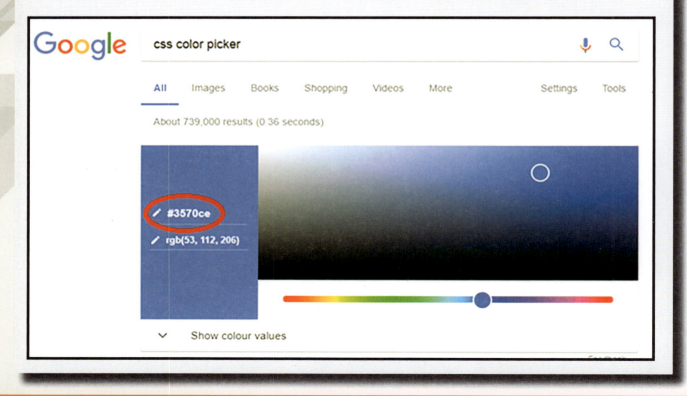

5. To make Steve's website look a bit more modern, we'll start by tweaking the **TOPBAR <DIV>**. If we type <div>, CSS will apply the changes to every <div> on the page, and we don't want that. Remember how we added an ID earlier? We can **SELECT AN ELEMENT WITH AN ID BY TYPING # BEFORE THE ID NAME.**

Try typing this into your CSS file before saving and reloading the website:

```
#topbar{

    min-height:300px;
    width:100%;
    background-color:white;

}
```

See how the topbar section changed? It's all white now! However, we have a lot of unused space, so let's make the text bigger and change its position.

6. Here, we have **"#TOPBAR P"**. This means that the CSS file looks for elements with the ID of "topbar", then applies the changes to any <p> tags inside it.

```
#topbar p{

    font-size:  6vmin;
    display:  inline-block;
    margin-top:6%;
    margin-left:10%;

}
```

Hi, I'm Steve! Welcome to my website!

WHO AM I?: I'm a miner!
WHAT DO I DO?: I build things and go on adventures!
MY FAVORITE THINGS ARE: Diamonds and exploring

TRY RESIZING YOUR BROWSER WINDOW. Notice how the topbar and its text change size? This is so your site looks great on any device, whether it's your phone, computer, or tablet. However, the picture pops out of the box when the screen is really small, so let's fix that.

7. We need to **TELL THE IMAGE TO STAY** on the left-hand side at all times. We also need to make it a little smaller, so it fits better.

```
#steve{

    float:left;
    margin-left:2%;
    margin-top:  5px;
    max-width:95%;
    max-height:95%;

}
```

Great, it stays put when on a tiny screen now! Try playing around with these numbers and see what happens.

8. It's time to **ADD THE FINISHING TOUCHES**. We want the mainsection <div> to match the top bar, and every other <p> tag to be larger. To do this, type the text below into your CSS file:

```
#mainsection{

    height: 60%;
    width: 90%;
    background-color: white;
    border-radius: 25px;
    margin-left: 5%;
    margin-top: 1%;


}
```

```
p{


    font-size: 4vmin;
    display: block;
    margin-left: 3%;
    margin-right: 3%;
    word-break: keep-all;


}
```

There are a couple of new things here. **THE BORDER-RADIUS PROPERTY** gives your <div> rounded corners and makes it look more modern. **THE WORD-BREAK ONE** helps so that your text isn't cut off mid-word on devices with small screens.

SIZE-WISE CODING ✕

Sometimes we've used percentages for width and height, and other times we've used "px" or pixels. Why is that? **Percentage values are great for elements that might change size!** Here, we've used it to allow for really long answers in the questions section. Try entering a huuuuge answer in the HTML document, save it, and reload the page. What happens?

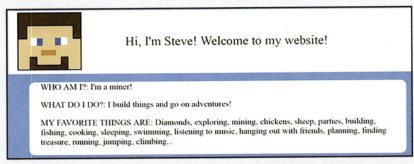

See how the box keeps getting bigger? If we'd used a pixel value here, the text would have leaked out onto the blue areas! This tells us that we should only use pixel values for objects that are supposed to stay a certain size.

9. Let's explore **ONE LAST ELEMENT** in this mission. In your CSS file, enter this under the #steve section:

```
transform: rotate(180deg);
```

Notice anything different? Steve is upside down now! Try entering different numbers here, and see what happens.

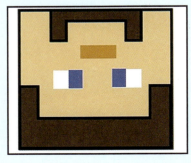

Once you're done, type two forward slashes in front of this line. **THIS IS CALLED A COMMENT, AND IT MAKES IT AS THOUGH YOU NEVER TYPED THAT LINE AT ALL.** This is useful for when you've added lots of CSS and can't tell which part is making things look strange. Instead of deleting the entire section, you can comment it out.

You can comment out lots of lines at once by typing a forward slash and a "*" symbol at the beginning, and the reverse at the end. Like this:

```
//This is a single line comment

/*
This is a
multi-line
comment
*/
```

You should know that HTML has its own way of commenting versus CSS. The good news is that there's only one way of doing it, no matter how many lines you need to comment out:

```
<!-- This is a single line comment in HTML-->

<!-- This is a multi-line
     comment in HTML -->
```

If you've made it this far, you've survived CSS! Keep playing around with CSS to learn more, and before you know it, you'll be a style master.

MISSION 3
HELLO, POP-UPS: GET JAZZY WITH JAVASCRIPT

If HTML builds the structure of a website and CSS makes the website look good, what does JavaScript (sometimes called JS) do? Basically, it lets us add cool features to a site and change the way people interact with it. Together, they make a winning team for a fun, easy-to-use website! Let's help Steve's site get a taste of JavaScript.

Think of JavaScript like redstone—it adds extra functionality to your already great creations!

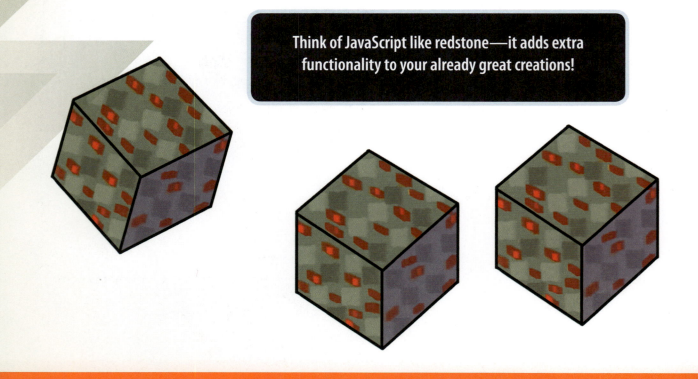

LET'S GET SET

I. It's time to add a couple of new tags to our HTML page. Underneath the line that says "</body>", and above the line that says "</html>", type **"<SCRIPT></SCRIPT>"**. Whenever we want to run some JavaScript, it has to go inside of these tags.

2. Next, we should get to know variables. **A VARIABLE IS SIMPLY A VALUE THAT WE STORE TO USE LATER.** This could be a number, some text, or even a list of other variables. To create a variable, type:
var VARIABLE_NAME_HERE = VARIABLE_VALUE_HERE

For instance:
var x = 5;

```
//These are valid variables

var x = 5;
var number = 5;
var xNumber = 5;
var X_Number = 5;

//These are not

var x number = 5;
var number! = 5;
```

Variable names can only be one word long. You can link several words together if you'd like, but try to keep things as simple as possible. Variables can be used for all sorts of things. Take a look at the code below, for instance, which creates a pop-up with the number 9:

```
var x = 5;
var y = 4;
window.alert(x+y);
```

READY TO GO!

3. Now that you know the basics, let's get started. **OPEN THE "INDEX" HTML FILE** you created for Steve's website in Mission 1. At the bottom of the file, between the closing body and closing html tags, type this:

```
<script>

    function sayHello(){
        var name = prompt("Hi, what's your name?");
        if(name !== null){
            window.alert("It's nice to meet you "+name+"! Thanks for checking out my website!");
        }
    }

</script>
```

THIS MINI-PROGRAM CALLED SAYHELLO ASKS THE USER FOR THEIR NAME. The name is stored in a variable, which you'll remember is just a number, piece of text, or list that we can use later. In this case, we use the variable to display the user's name in a pop-up.

4. The first thing to look at here is the **"IF(NAME !== NULL)"** part. This is called an IF statement. Simply, if the thing inside the brackets happens, the code underneath will run. If not, it won't. So what do we have inside our IF statement this time?

```
//Notice how the text in speech marks is light grey? Your variables should always be a different color
window.alert("It's nice to meet you "+name+"! Thanks for checking out my website!");
```

In JavaScript, an exclamation mark (!) means not. "!==" means not equal to. Here, "null" means that no text was entered.

So, if the name entered is not equal to null, run the next part. As long as someone types a name in, the next section will run.

All text must be in quotation marks. If you want to use a variable, you need to close the quotation marks first, then use a + sign; otherwise, it won't work.

5. Now that we've created a function, we need to **TELL THE WEBSITE WHEN TO RUN IT**. Underneath your <p> tags, enter this:

```
<button id= 'mainbutton' type='button' onclick = sayHello()>Say Hi!</button>
```

THE TEXT BETWEEN THE <BUTTON> TAGS IS WHAT THE BUTTON WILL ACTUALLY SAY.
Feel free to change this if you'd like to. When you're ready, refresh the page and click the button.

You should see a box like this. If you understood the code, you already know what's going to happen when you type your name in. Try it now!

> From this page
>
> It's nice to meet you Ian! Thanks for checking out my website!
>
> OK

Great, it looks like our function works perfectly! But our button looks ugly, doesn't it? Let's spice it up with a little bit of CSS.

6. OPEN YOUR CSS FILE for Steve's website and enter the following code at the bottom:

```css
#mainbutton{

    margin-left: 5%;
    margin-bottom:2%;
    background-color: #4CAF50;
    color: white;
    padding: 15px 20px;
    display: inline-block;
    font-size: 24px;

}
```

Save it, then reload the site to see how it looks. That's better!

AHEAD, PLAY!   X

As part of this mission, you can change the margins to move the button around, update the font size to make the text larger, and vary the padding to make the button bigger. Why not make this button your favorite color? Remember, it's the "color" option, followed by either a color name or hex value (turn back to page 10 if you need some hints).

We got a good start on JavaScript with a peek into what you can do with variables. If you're ready for more JavaScript, you're ready for Mission 4. Just wait until you uncover all you can do with loops!

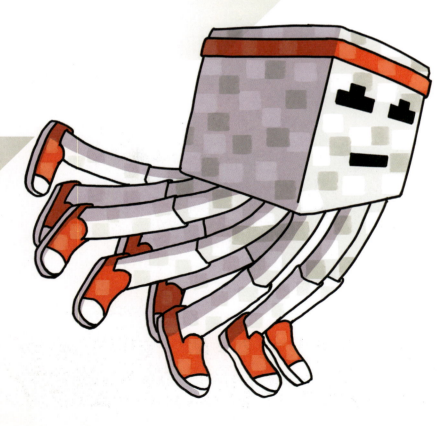

MISSION 4
GO EXPLORING: MAKE IT EASY WITH LOOPS

Learning your first bits of JavaScript with variables was pretty cool, wasn't it? But JavaScript can be used for far more than just making pop-ups! In Mission 4, we're bringing loops into the picture to expand the possibilities. So what is a loop? A loop is a kind of smart shortcut that lets you run the same piece of code lots of times without making you type it out over and over again.

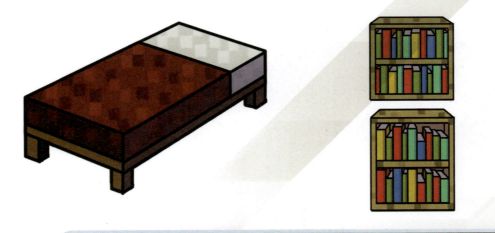

Loops give you a quick and easy way to do something repeatedly.
Don't you wish you could create a loop for cleaning your room?

LET'S GET SET

I. Once you see **HOW LOOPS WORK**, you'll find that they're amazing but simple:

```
for( variable_starting_number; variable_ending_number; how_much_to_increase_variable_each_time){

//this is where you put the code you want to run over and over

}
```

Try typing this example into your <script> tags:

```
for(i=1; i<6; i++){
    window.alert("This is popup number "+i);
}
```

In this case, our variable is called "i" and it starts with a value of 1. See the last part? "i++" means that the loop adds 1 to our variable every time it runs the code. You could also use "i = i+1" if you like. The loop runs as long as the variable i is less than 6. In this example, it runs five times.

Now, you should know what the code inside the brackets does. It creates a pop-up with the current value of i in it. Since the loop runs five times, when you reload your page, you should see five pop-ups one after the other. Easy, right?

From this page

This is popup number 1

OK

From this page

This is popup number 2

OK

From this page

This is popup number 3

OK

From this page

This is popup number 4

OK

From this page

This is popup number 5

OK

Okay, go ahead and delete this code now. Then we can explore how to use loops on Steve's website!

2. What if we made a function that randomly chooses things from a list? To do this, we'll need to know something about arrays. **ARRAYS ARE ANOTHER KIND OF VARIABLE.** They're basically just lists, but you can do some really cool things with them, as we'll see shortly.

You can put almost anything inside an array! Let's take a look at a few examples:

```
var firstArray = [1,2,3,4,5];
var secondArray = ["You", "Can", "Store", "Words", "Too!"];

var x = 5;
var y = 10;
var z = 15;

var thirdArray = [x,y,z];
var fourthArray = [1, "You", x];
```

Hurray for Arrays   X

In the examples, did you notice how **you can mix and match the different variable types inside an array**? As long as you type a comma after each item, there's no problem! Arrays are like houses—you can have lots of different things inside, as long as it's all organized properly.

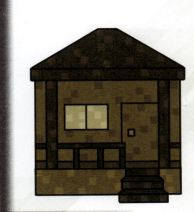

One of the cool things about arrays is that you can grab specific items from them. You tell your script that you want the first (or second, or third) element from the array. One thing to note: arrays start at zero, so to get the first item, you'd ask for "myFirstArray[0]". To get the second, you'd ask for "myFirstArray[1]", and so on.

READY TO GO!

2. First, open your HTML file. Underneath the buttons (and inside the main-section <div> tags) in your HTML document, **ADD ANOTHER SET OF <DIV> TAGS, WITH AN ID OF "LOOP–SECTION"**. Add another button, too, using this code:

```
<button id= 'mainbutton' type='button' onclick = explore()>Go Exploring!</button>
```

3. We're going to be using something called **JQUERY TO ADD NEW ITEMS** to the page. Up in the <head> section, add the following line:

```
<script src="https://ajax.googleapis.com/ajax/libs/jquery/3.3.1/jquery.min.js"></script>
```

jQuery is a really big file, so instead of downloading it, this line just tells your page where to find it on the Internet.

4. Our button says it's going to run **A FUNCTION CALLED "EXPLORE()"** when clicked, so let's create that now. Do you remember how to start building a function?

```
function explore(){

}
```

Now we'll **CREATE A COUPLE OF ARRAYS**. In the first one, type a few of your favorite Minecraft locations, and in the second one, a few things you might find when out exploring.

```
function explore(){

    var locations = ['an old, spooky temple', 'a village', 'an underwater palace', 'a deep, dark cave', 'a huge pyramid'];

    var items = ['a diamond','a pumpkin','a golden apple', 'a creeper', 'lots of bats', 'treasure', 'an iron helmet', 'some coal'];

}
```

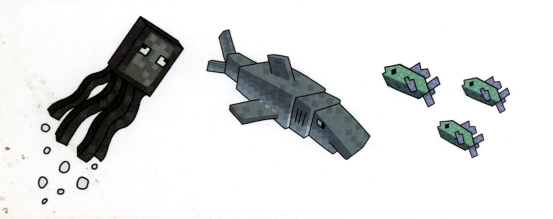

Next, we'll add some **CODE TO CHOOSE A RANDOM LOCATION** from the array:

```
var chosenLocation = locations[Math.floor(Math.random()*locations.length)];
```

This looks a bit confusing, but it works by checking how many things are stored in the *locations* array, then choosing a random whole number between zero and the length of the array.

5. You can change various parts of your website with JavaScript. Below, we'll use code to **GET RID OF ALL THE TEXT IN THE "LOOP-SECTION"** whenever the "Go Exploring!" button is clicked.

```
document.getElementById("loop-section").innerHTML = "";
```

Here's the exciting bit! Let's **USE JQUERY TO ADD THE RANDOM LOCATION** from earlier onto our web page:

```
$('#loop-section').append("<p>I went exploring earlier and found "+chosenLocation+". Inside I found: </p>
```

Save your document, then reload the website and **CLICK THE "GO EXPLORING!" BUTTON**. What happens? What happens if you click it a lot of times?

```
  Say Hi!        Go Exploring!

  I went exploring earlier and found an old, spooky temple. Inside I found:
```

Do you see how the text changes? This is because **WHENEVER YOU CLICK THE BUTTON, YOUR EXPLORE() FUNCTION CHOOSES A NEW RANDOM PLACE FROM THE ARRAY!** You might notice that you sometimes get the same results, though. This is because we only have a few places to choose from. Why not add some more?

6. Now we're going to **USE A LOOP TO CHOOSE THREE ITEMS** from our *items* array and display them.

```
for (i = 1; i < 4; i++) {

    var foundItem = items[Math.floor(Math.random()*items.length)];

    $('#loop-section').append("<p>"+foundItem+", </p>");

}
```

What happens if you click the button now?

> I went exploring earlier and found an underwater palace. Inside I found:
>
> a creeper,   a diamond,   a pumpkin,

That's pretty good, but it doesn't look quite right! Let's get rid of the $('#loop-section') line and add an IF statement to take care of that last comma. Do you see how we've used two equals signs in the IF statement? In JavaScript, you only use a single equals sign when creating or changing variables.

```javascript
if(i==3){
    $('#loop-section').append("<p>and "+foundItem+"</p>");
}else{
    $('#loop-section').append("<p>"+foundItem+", </p>");
}
```

Get it? If *i = 3*, the item doesn't have a comma after it. Instead, it has the word "and" before it. Okay, so *now* how does it look?

> I went exploring earlier and found an underwater palace. Inside I found:
>
> an iron helmet,   a diamond,   and lots of bats

Nice work! You've just created a JavaScript function that uses variables, loops, and IF statements. Fun fact: you can use these techniques to make almost anything you can imagine. Can you think of something else you could build with variables, loops, and IF statements?

MISSION 5

PLAY WITH STEVE: SET UP A STORYTELLING GAME

Anyone coming to Steve's website will probably expect a game to be included. It's easier than you think to set something up! Let's see what we can do by putting together some simple coding concepts we've gone through together so far. Every classic game starts somewhere, so let's put our minds and some coding together.

You can create code to generate random adventures! Just follow the steps.

LET'S GET SET

1. First, we need a way for website visitors to find and play the game. Open up your HTML file again. Remember how we created a button before? **ADD ANOTHER BUTTON** underneath the others, and **MAKE IT RUN A FUNCTION CALLED PLAYGAME()** when clicked. You should also make the button say "Play a Game!"

```
<button id= 'mainbutton' type='button' onclick = playGame()>Play a Game!</button>
```

2. Now **WE'LL SET UP THAT FUNCTION**. Remember to put this part inside the <script> tags at the bottom. We want to get some information from the user. We're going to ask them for their favorite Minecraft character and their favorite monster. Do you remember how to do this?

```
function playGame(){

var favCharacter = prompt("Who is your favorite Minecraft character?");

var favMonster = prompt("What is your favorite Minecraft monster?");

}
```

From this page

Who is your favorite Minecraft character?

Steve

OK   Cancel

From this page

What is your favorite Minecraft monster?

Creeper

OK   Cancel

3. We'll need to create a basic story using pop-ups. First, though, we have to **MAKE SURE THAT THE USER ACTUALLY ENTERED NAMES FOR BOTH A CHARACTER AND A MONSTER**. In this case, "IF(favCharacter && favMonster)" checks to see if these variables are empty or not. Notice that we've used two "&" signs here—JavaScript won't accept just one.

```
var build = window.prompt(favCharacter+ " is in a new area and it's getting dark! What should they build? Type bed, house, or nothing")

if(build == "nothing"){

    window.alert(favCharacter+" spends their day playing and has to run from "+favMonster+"s at night. Try again!");

}
```

4. For the game itself, we can **GIVE THE USER A CHOICE OF THINGS TO BUILD, THEN MAKE A STORY BASED ON THE RESULTS**. Remember, you don't have to use this story; yours can be as simple or advanced as you like.

```javascript
function playGame(){

    var favCharacter = prompt("Who is your favorite Minecraft character?");

    var favMonster = prompt("What is your favorite Minecraft monster?");

    if(favCharacter && favMonster){

    }
}
```

See how this takes the user's choice and uses it to change the program? Shall we add a few more options? By adding the code below into the IF statement, we can take care of people who choose to build a bed first.

```javascript
if(build == "bed"){

    window.alert(favCharacter+" builds a bed and goes to sleep. They wake up surrounded by "+favMonster+"s! Try again!");

}
```

Okay, both of these options have led to a game over! What if we want to move the story forward? We need to **NEST IF STATEMENTS.** This means we put one IF statement inside another to let us ask for specific circumstances.

```javascript
if(build == "house"){

    window.alert(favCharacter+ " builds themselves a nice, cosy house to keep the "+favMonster+"s out.");
    wolf = window.prompt("A wolf appears! Does "+favCharacter+" run or try to tame it?");

    if(wolf == "tame"){

        window.alert(favCharacter+" tames the wolf! It keeps them safe from monsters. Good job!");

    }else{

        window.alert(favCharacter+" runs from the wolf and has to leave the house behind! Try again!");

    }

}
```

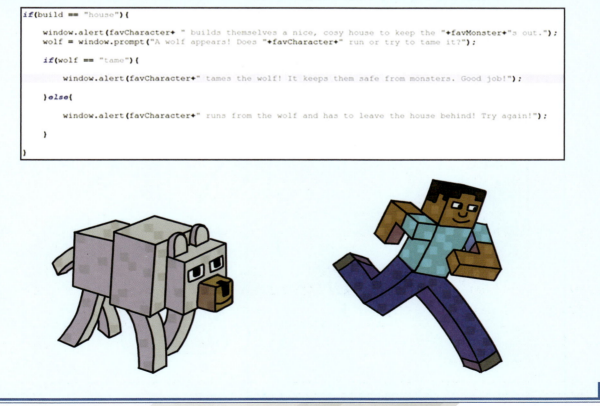

There's something new in here! Did you notice that the wolf's **IF STATEMENT SAYS ELSE UNDERNEATH**? This means that if the user types "tame", the code in the IF part runs. But if they type anything else, the code in the ELSE part runs. This code is great for when you want the user to choose between several options.

Ready for even more options in the world of coding? Our adventures in animation start next!

ANIMATION ADVENTURES

Mission 1
Characters Welcome: Create Assets for Animation

Before we can animate anything through coding, we need to find or create the characters to bring to life. It's an extra bit of fun we can have with a computer-drawing program before we dive into code! The characters we are going to create can be called *assets*, if you want to impress your friends. Assets are simply things such as images and audio files that are used with your website or program.

Which comes first: the chicken or the egg? In this mission, it's the chicken with a creeper in between!

1. Open up your **FAVORITE DRAWING PROGRAM**. Begin by drawing a Minecraft chicken. Make sure to draw it from the side—a front view won't work for what we're going to do. Use a big rectangle for the body, then add the smaller details such as the head and wing.

2. Once you've drawn the chicken, it's time to color it! Remember to make the picture as small as possible without cutting off any parts of the chicken—often called cropping. You can do this by clicking the squares that appear when you click outside of your image.

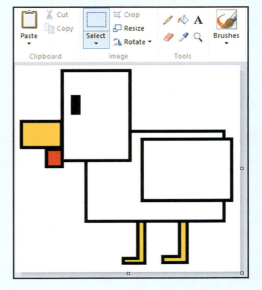

3. Now, it's time to save your file. What file format should you use? Well, **PNG FILES** look better, but too many can make your website load slowly. So for now, we'll stick with **JPG FILES**. Save the picture as **"CHICKEN.JPG"** and put it into the same folder as your HTML page.

4. Next, it's back to the drawing board to **CREATE A CREEPER** instead of a chicken. This time, though, we want to draw a creeper that's looking straight at you! This character's easy to draw: just **USE THE RECTANGLE** tool to make the outline and face. Next, add some differently colored squares and rectangles to its body to give it a real Minecraft feel.

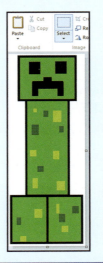

5. After your creeper creation is complete, save the file as **"CREEPER.JPG"**, remembering to put it into the same folder as the last image.

6. Okay, we're almost at the asset finish line! All that's missing is a chicken egg. To make it easy, you can **USE THE CIRCLE TOOL TO CREATE A PERFECT EGG SHAPE**. The circle tool should be in the toolbar, next to the other shape tools. This toolbar might be at the top, or at one of the sides, depending on which drawing program you're using. (In Microsoft Paint, it's at the top of the screen.)

7. Once your egg has hatched from your drawing program, save it as **"EGG.JPG"**.

Now that you've created such amazing assets, we can have fun with coding movement for our Minecraft characters in Mission 2 (page 35). They're ready to go when you are!

Z SHORTCUT TO KNOW   X

Don't worry if you make any mistakes! You can quickly get rid of them by pressing the **Control key** and **Z** at the same time. This is a shortcut for the **Undo** feature. But what if you accidentally undo something you wanted to keep? No problem: **Redo** it by combining the **Control key** and **Y**.

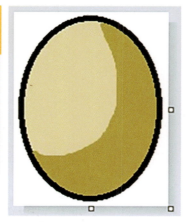

Mission 2
Chicken Versus Creeper: Code a Web Animation

Ready to make your animation really come alive? It's time to discover how to add fun movement. You can give all kinds of commands through just a little code. We can start with a chicken and creeper, and see where our commands lead them. Once you get the hang of it, who knows where your coding will take you and your animated characters!

Why did the chicken cross the creeper? Because you told it to with coding!

LET'S GET SET

1. Now that our web page has grown, we can put our animations on a separate page. Add another button next to the ones you made earlier with this code:

```
<button id="mainbutton" onclick="location.href='animation.html'">Watch animation</button>
```

Got it? The **"LOCATION.HREF"** part says which page to go to. If you want to create a link without making it a button, you could also use this code:

```
<a href = animation.html>Watch Animation</a>
```

2. But wait: we don't have a page with that name! No problem—let's create one. Go ahead and click **FILE**, then **NEW** and save it as **"ANIMATION.HTML"**. Next, we'll copy some code over so that this page matches the style of the home page:

```
<!DOCTYPE html>
<html>

<head>
<link rel="stylesheet" type="text/css" href="style.css">
<script src="https://ajax.googleapis.com/ajax/libs/jquery/3.3.1/jquery.min.js"></script>
</head>

<body>

    <div id='topbar'>
        <img id ='steve' src='steve.jpg'/>
        <p> Hi, I'm Steve! Welcome to my website! </p>
    </div>

    <div id='mainsection'>

    </div>

</body>
</html>
```

READY TO GO!

3. Okay, let's start simple. Why don't we put our picture of a chicken onto the site? To do this, enter this little bit of code into the "mainsection" div:

```
<img id = 'chicken' class = 'chickenAnimation' src = 'chicken.jpg'/>
```

Notice the **CLASS PROPERTY**? Classes are similar to IDs, but instead of targeting one object at a time, they're designed to **TARGET** lots of things all at once! In our case, we're going to use classes to stop the chicken's animation later on.

4. Our chicken is ready. It's time to go over your CSS file and add a new line at the bottom. Now, our image has the ID "chicken", so how do we **TARGET** it? That's right, with the **# SYMBOL**. With this in mind, we can make a few adjustments to the image:

```
#chicken{

    border-radius:25px;
    max-width:10%;
    max-height: 20%;
}

.chickenAnimation{

    -webkit-animation: walk 6s infinite;

}
```

5. We know that the border radius gives the image rounded corners, but what about that line in the bottom section? Basically, it tells the website how to animate our image. The first part is the **NAME OF OUR ANIMATION FUNCTION**, the second is **HOW LONG THE ANIMATION SHOULD TAKE** in seconds, and the last part says **HOW MANY TIMES THE ANIMATION SHOULD HAPPEN**. Infinite just means that the animation will loop forever.

Let's make the **"WALK" ANIMATION FUNCTION**. Type the following code into your CSS file:

```
@keyframes walk {

    50%   { margin-left: 80%;}
    100%  { margin-left: 0%;}
}
```

Notice how the parts inside the brackets are just standard CSS? This means you can control the time that certain effects happen by typing them in here. You can even do multiple things at the same time by separating them with a semicolon (;).

SEE THE PERCENTAGES? THINK OF THESE LIKE STEPS. Here, step one is to move the image to the right, and step two is to move it back. Try saving your HTML and CSS files, then reloading the page. The chicken should now move!

6. Our chicken looks okay, but not perfect just yet because the chicken is always facing the same way. We can change that by **FLIPPING** it with one line of code!

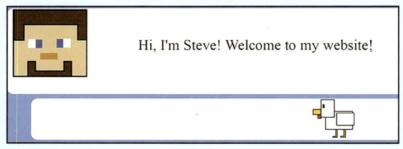

Because our chicken was facing the wrong direction, we first flip it to face the right-hand side. Next, it moves over to the right, then flips again. Finally, it moves back to the left and faces the right again. Easy, right?

```
#creeper{

    max-width:8%;

}
```

There's so much more you can do with keyframes! Have a little fun with some of the ideas in "Crazy for Commands" on page 40.

7. Let's try adding another image. This time, insert the picture you drew of a creeper, and give it the ID "creeper". Depending on how big your image is, you might notice that it goes off the screen. To fix this, we'll **ADD SOME CSS**.

```
@keyframes walk {

    0% {transform: scaleX(-1);}
    20% { margin-left: 80%; }
    60% { transform: scaleX(1);}
    80% { margin-left: 0%;}
    100% {transform: scaleX(-1);}

}
```

Try changing the number here until the creeper fits perfectly. Something strange is happening, though. Notice how the creeper runs back and forward even though it doesn't have the animation part in its CSS? This is because the chicken image automatically pushes things away when it moves!

The good news is that this does most of the work for us. Now it looks like the chicken and creeper are taking turns chasing each other! Isn't that cool? Great job on your web animation mission!

CRAZY FOR COMMANDS   X

Try entering the following commands at different steps of the animation. You might also want to see what difference changing the percentage numbers makes. Have fun experimenting!

What do the following commands do?

- transform: rotateY(270deg);

- max-height: 100px;

- opacity: 0.1;

- transform: skewY(50deg);

The best thing about keyframe animations is that you can apply them to whatever you like, not just images. Try copying and pasting the "-webkit-animation" CSS from the chicken to another element. What happens? Of course, you'll want to remove this afterward since too much movement can be pretty distracting!

MISSION 3
CHICKEN RESCUE: GIVE YOUR ANIMATION A SPIN

Whew! Your chicken has been on the run for some time now, thanks to a successful Mission 2. But we all know what will happen if the creeper catches up to the chicken. Shall we help it out? Interactive features you code can come to the rescue to keep your chicken and eggs safe.

Running chickens are funny, but we'd rather see creepers defeated by coding!

READY TO GO!

1. We're going to **ADD A NEW ANIMATION** in the CSS file. This one is **CALLED "SPIN"** and will make the creeper spin around. It's really simple:

```
@keyframes spin {

    0% {transform: rotate(0deg);}
    100% {transform: rotate(360deg);}


}
```

2. Next, we'll apply a class to the creeper. When it's clicked, it gets all the properties of the class. In this case, the class makes it spin around. Remember how we used "#" to select IDs in CSS? **TO SELECT A CLASS, YOU ENTER A PERIOD.** For instance:

```
.defeated{

    -webkit-animation: spin 0.1s 3;

}
```

Add this code, then save the CSS file.

3. Now, open up your animation.html page again. Add some **<SCRIPT> TAGS** at the bottom of the page between the </body> and </html> tags.

4. It's time to **USE JQUERY** again! This time, we'll be telling it to apply the .defeated class when the creeper is clicked.

```
<script>

$('#creeper').click(function(){

    $('#creeper').addClass('defeated');

});

</script>
```

If you refresh your web page and click the creeper, you'll **SEE HIM SPIN AROUND**!

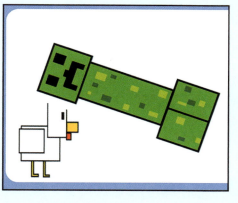

Okay, but that doesn't help the chicken, does it? So let's also **GET RID OF THE CREEPER**!

```
$('#creeper').click(function(){

    $('#creeper').addClass('defeated');
    $('#creeper').remove();
});
```

Try clicking the creeper again. There's a problem—it disappears immediately and we don't see it spin around. We can fix this issue.

5. Let's add a **TIMER**, which allows us to say exactly when we want a specific thing to happen. For instance, we want to wait until the creeper is finished spinning before we delete it.

```
<script>

$('#creeper').click(function(){

    $('#creeper').addClass('defeated');

    window.setTimeout(function(){

        $('#creeper').remove();

    }, 350);

});

</script>
```

See how we added code into the **"SETTIMEOUT" FUNCTION**? It looks strange, though, doesn't it? What's the number after it for? Well, that is the number of milliseconds we want to wait before running the code inside the function. One second is 1,000 milliseconds, so we're waiting a little over ⅓ of a second—just enough time for the creeper to stop spinning.

6. Now that the creeper's gone, the chicken has nothing to worry about! It can stop running around. To make this happen, we'll **REMOVE THE "CHICKENANIMATION" CLASS AND PAUSE THE ANIMATION** by adding two extra lines of code:

```
window.setTimeout(function(){

    $('#creeper').remove();
    $("#chicken").removeClass( "chickenAnimation" );
    $("#chicken").css("-webkit-animation-play-state", "pause");

}, 350);
```

Notice how the chicken stops being animated and returns to just being a normal image. Of course, if a chicken stays in one place for a long time, that usually means it's about to lay an egg. Can we make that happen? You bet!

7. Let's break this down as simply as possible. When the chicken is clicked, we want an egg to appear. So we'll **MAKE A FUNCTION** that does this:

```
$('#chicken').click(function(){

    $('#mainsection').append("<img class = 'egg' src='egg.jpeg'/>");

})
```

Since we might have multiple eggs, we'll use **A CLASS INSTEAD OF AN ID**. In your CSS file, make sure your egg class has a "max-width" and "max-height" that are realistic (we used "max-width: 2%" and max-height: 4%"). After all, you can't have an egg bigger than the chicken that laid it!

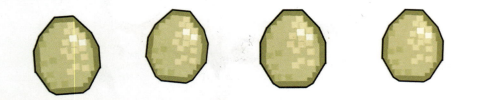

There's one more problem. A chicken won't lay eggs if it doesn't feel safe. Right now, it will lay an egg whenever you click it, even if the creeper is still chasing it.

Accidental Asset   X

Did you know the creeper was created by a coding accident? It's true: Minecraft creator Markus "Notch" Persson was planning to code a pig when the height and width got switched. Suddenly, there was this Minecraft character that was tall instead of long, with little feet. **Coding experiments can be fun**—and even become history!

8. We need to make sure the chicken only lays eggs if the creeper is gone. The best way to accomplish our goal? **USE JQUERY!** JQuery lets you check how many things have a certain class or ID. Here, we'll use it to tell us **HOW MANY ITEMS HAVE THE "CREEPER" ID.** If any exist, the length checker will say how many. If no item has that ID, it will return a value of 0. Since the creeper is removed when clicked, we need our chicken to only lay eggs if there are no creepers on the page.

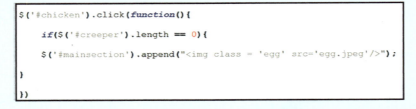

```
$('#chicken').click(function(){

    if($('#creeper').length == 0){

    $('#mainsection').append("<img class = 'egg' src='egg.jpeg'/>");

}

})
```

SAVE YOUR FILES AND RELOAD the animation page. Try clicking on the chicken first: notice how it doesn't lay any eggs? Now click the creeper to get rid of it, then try clicking the chicken again.

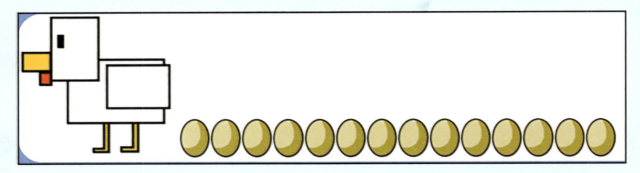

Goal accomplished! Better yet, if you click the chicken a bunch of times, you'll notice that the eggs never break out of the mainsection <div>. Eggs-cellent coding work!

MISSION 4

AMAZING EGG EFFECTS: PLAYING WITH PLUGINS

O f course, Minecraft eggs are useful to collect—and sometimes even throw. They can also be fun when you code cool effects for them, from bounce and drop to shake and slide. By adding another jQuery plugin called jQuery UI, let's discover all the interesting stuff we can make happen through coding!

Think gold or diamond tools are powerful? You haven't tried this tool: a jQuery plugin.

LET'S GET SET

1. ADD THIS LINE to the <head> section of your animation page:

```
<script src="https://ajax.googleapis.com/ajax/libs/jqueryui/1.12.1/jquery-ui.min.js"></script>
```

So what does jQuery UI let us do?

READY TO GO!

2. Let's see what happens if we **ADD THIS CODE** to the #chicken.click() function:

```
$('.egg').draggable();
```

You can now click and drag on each egg! Try it—drag some of the eggs around the page.

3. What else? You can also **ADD COOL EFFECTS** to elements.

```
$('.egg:last-child').effect( "bounce", "slow" );
```

If we add the code above, each egg will bounce when it appears! That's not the only effect, though. Try replacing the effect with the following:

- "shake"
- "drop"
- "puff"
- "pulsate"
- "slide"

You can even **CHANGE THE SPEED** if you'd like. What happens if you change "slow" to "fast"?

4. You can **RESIZE WITH JQUERY UI**, too. However, to do this, you have to add another CSS sheet in the <head> tags. Type this in there:

```
<link rel="stylesheet" href="https://ajax.googleapis.com/ajax/libs/jqueryui/1.12.1/themes/smoothness/jquery-ui.css">
```

Once this is done, you can make any element resizable by using the **.RESIZABLE() FUNCTION** inside <script> tags. Here's an example:

```
$('p').resizable();
```

Now any HTML paragraph should have an arrow in the bottom-right corner. Try dragging this arrow to make the paragraph larger or smaller. It's important to note that changing the size of the chicken, egg, or creeper will mess up the animation, but almost anything else can be changed without any issues.

5. Finally, we'll investigate jQuery UI's **DROPPABLE() FUNCTION**. This function allows us to do specific things when an item is dropped into a certain area. Here's one idea of how we can put it to work.

When a chicken lays an egg, you don't want to just leave it! Instead, you want to pick it up, right? Why don't we **TURN THE TOPBAR <DIV> INTO SOMETHING USEFUL**? We can have it keep count of how many eggs are dropped there.

First, we have to **CREATE A VARIABLE CALLED EGGCOUNT**. We'll set this to zero.

```
var eggCount = 0;
```

6. Next, we'll **MAKE THE TOPBAR <DIV> DROPPABLE**. This means we can tell if a draggable item is dropped here.

```
$('#topbar').droppable({

});
```

7. Okay, we have to **TELL THE TOPBAR WHAT TO DO** when something is dropped in now. To do this, we'll create a function inside this piece of code:

```
$('#topbar').droppable({
    drop: function(){

    }
});
```

Whoa, that's a lot of brackets! Don't worry, though, there's not much left to do.

8. When an egg is dropped into our topbar <div>, we want to **INCREASE THE VALUE OF THE EGGCOUNT VARIABLE** by one.

```
eggCount = eggCount+1;
```

9. Finally, **CHANGE THE TOPBAR TEXT** to say how many eggs there are. It's the only paragraph on the page, right? So all we have to do is select the paragraphs with jQuery and change what they say.

```
$('#topbar').droppable({
    drop: function(){
        eggCount = eggCount+1;
        $("p").html("There are "+eggCount+" eggs in the top bar");
    }
});
```

Remember that if we had more than one paragraph, the text would change for all of them, though. To prevent this, we'd select all elements with the "topbar" ID.

Okay, now **SAVE THIS AND RELOAD THE PAGE**. Can you see what the problem is? When you drag an egg into the topbar, then remove it, the counter stays the same. Then when you drag the same egg back, it increases the counter again. Don't worry—this is an easy fix.

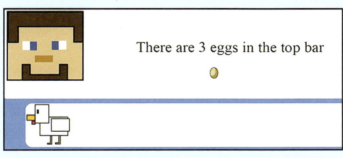

10. All we need to do is **TELL THE PROGRAM TO TAKE ONE AWAY** from the egg-Count variable whenever an egg leaves the top bar. We only have to copy and paste the function we just made, but instead of adding 1 to the counter, we subtract! Also, change the word "drop" to the word "out".

```
$( "#topbar" ).droppable({
    out: function() {
        eggCount = eggCount-1;
        $("p").html("There are "+eggCount+" eggs in the top bar");
    }
});
```

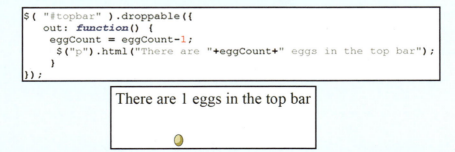

That's almost perfect! We just need to **ADD AN IF STATEMENT** to both functions so we can fix the grammar:

```
if(eggCount == 1){

    $("p").html("There is "+eggCount+" egg in the top bar");

}else{

    $("p").html("There are "+eggCount+" eggs in the top bar");

}
```

There is 1 egg in the top bar

Coding Detective   X

Did you discover a few glitches with your egg counter? First, if you try to drag an egg before its animation has finished, it might not move where you want. Second, dragging one egg back and forth inside the top bar increases the counter. The solutions to these problems are pretty complicated, though, so for now we'll move on. Can you think of a way to prevent these issues? **Coding often takes trying new ideas and approaches** to get the exact results you want—it's a challenge coders love!

MAKING MUSIC

MISSION 1
NOTES WITH STEVE: BUILD AN ONLINE PIANO

One of the great things about coding and web design is that you can customize almost every little thing. So far, we've focused on making our website for Steve look good. But you can fill it with sounds, too. To get started, we're going to create a simple online piano!

The creepers are ready to rock! Let's add some music to Steve's site.

LET'S GET SET

I. We'll put this on a separate page, just like with the animation. **OPEN UP YOUR INDEX.HTML** file in a TextEditor and **ADD A NEW BUTTON** that links to a page called "music.html". You can copy and paste the code for the animation button if you like, but remember to change the page address and button text.

```html
<button id="mainbutton" onclick="location.href='music.html'">Play Music</button>
```

2. Now, let's create the music page. Open a new document, type the following text, and **SAVE IT AS "MUSIC.HTML".** Make sure it's in the same folder as all your other HTML files.

```html
<!DOCTYPE html>
<html>

<head>
    <link rel="stylesheet" type="text/css" href="style.css">

</head>

<body>

<div id='topbar'>
    <img id ='steve' src='assets/steve.jpg'/>
    <p> Hi, I'm Steve! Welcome to the music page!</p>

</div>


<div id='mainsection'>

</div>

</body>

<script>

</script>

</html>
```

All this code does is set up the page with our top bar and main sections. There's another thing we need to do before we can really get started, though: a little more drawing!

3. When you want to make music in Minecraft, what do you build? If you aren't lucky enough to find CDs, you can always make some note blocks. Let's do that: Open up your drawing program, and **MAKE A PICTURE OF A NOTE BLOCK**. Remember to get rid of as much white space as possible, and when you're done, **NAME THE FILE "NOTE.JPG"**.

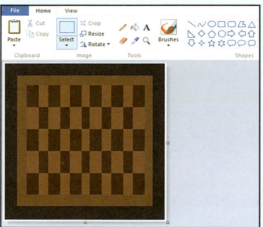

4. Okay, now let's **PUT THIS IMAGE ONTO OUR MUSIC PAGE**! Of course, it wouldn't be much of a piano if we only had one key, would it? Let's put this same image onto the page five times.

```
<div id='mainsection'>
    <img class = 'noteblock' id='note1' src = 'note.jpg'/>
    <img class = 'noteblock' id='note2' src = 'note.jpg'/>
    <img class = 'noteblock' id='note3' src = 'note.jpg'/>
    <img class = 'noteblock' id='note4' src = 'note.jpg'/>
    <img class = 'noteblock' id='note5' src = 'note.jpg'/>
</div>
```

You'll notice that each block has the "noteblock" class. If we **ADD A FEW LINES TO OUR CSS FILE**, we can make sure these boxes never go off the screen or mess up the layout of the page:

```
.noteblock{

    float:left;
    margin-left:4%;
    width:15%;
    max-height:50%;

}
```

Feel free to change the margin sizes, width, and height if you like! These sizes are just a general guideline, but if you want your note blocks to be larger or smaller, that's not a problem.

DID YOU KNOW?   X

The background music for Minecraft was recorded by a German electronic composer named Daniel Rosenfeld, aka "C418." His assistant was his pet cat, the same animal that provided the sounds used for the ghast.

READY TO GO!

5. There are a few different ways to **ADD MUSIC** to your website. The easiest way is to use the **<AUDIO> TAGS**, as shown below:

```
<audio src="music.mp3" autoplay>
</audio>
```

If you **REPLACE "MUSIC.MP3" WITH THE NAME OF A MUSIC FILE**, it'll start playing automatically when you reload the page. You can replace the "autoplay" part with "controls" if you want to be able to play or pause the music.

You can also use JavaScript plugins for greater control over when the music plays. However, these can be pretty complicated and don't always work perfectly.

6. So how can we **CREATE SOUNDS IF WE DON'T HAVE ANY MUSIC FILES** on our computer? Well, it's a bit trickier but definitely not impossible. We're going to use something called the **WEB AUDIO API**, a fairly new feature that lets us create any sound we'd like.

Put a set of <script> tags in the <head> section. Inside these, enter:

```
<script>
    var context = new AudioContext()
</script>
```

7. The next step takes a bit of background to understand. Have you ever wondered why functions always have brackets after them (sayHello(), for example)? It's because you can actually pass certain values to a function to help it run! That sounds complicated, so let's look at an example:

```
<script>

    showNumber(5);

    function showNumber(number){

        window.alert("You entered "+number);

    }

</script>
```

In this case, we call the showNumber function with a value of five. This function automatically creates a variable called "number" and sets it to five, then makes a pop-up with that number. Easy, right?

So what does this have to do with music? Well, go to the <script> tags at the bottom of the page. We're going to **CREATE A FUNCTION THAT PLAYS A DIFFERENT NOTE BASED ON THE NUMBER YOU ENTER!**

Start by entering the code below. Try not to worry about what these parts mean—this code is just what we need to set up the Web Audio API.

```
function playNote(frequency){

    var o = context.createOscillator()
    var  g = context.createGain()
    o.connect(g)
    g.connect(context.destination)

    o.start(0);

    o.frequency.value = frequency;

}
```

8. Now we can **ADD THE ONCLICK PART** to our note block images.

```
<img class = 'noteblock' onclick=playNote(130) src = 'note.jpg'/>
<img class = 'noteblock' onclick=playNote(146) src = 'note.jpg'/>
<img class = 'noteblock' onclick=playNote(164) src = 'note.jpg'/>
<img class = 'noteblock' onclick=playNote(174) src = 'note.jpg'/>
<img class = 'noteblock' onclick=playNote(195) src = 'note.jpg'/>
```

When you click a note block, a hum will sound. Why did we choose these numbers, though? Well, because they sound nice! If you try changing these numbers, you'll see how difficult it can be to get all the blocks in tune. Remember: low numbers make low sounds, and high numbers make high sounds.

There's a bit of a problem, though: these notes play forever, so it's difficult to play any kind of music. Let's **ADD TWO MORE LINES OF CODE** to fix this:

```
var notelength = 5;

g.gain.exponentialRampToValueAtTime(0.00001, context.currentTime + notelength)
```

There are two variables we can change here. The first is **NOTELENGTH**, which decides how long each note should play in seconds. The second is the other number in red, which decides how long each note should take to **FADE OUT**. See how it's really small? That's because we want a nice, short note.

So now we have some basic sound. But why stop there? Let's jazz up the options in Making Music, Mission 2!

Mission 2
Spice Up the Sounds: Add Audio Effects

In Mission 1, we built a really simple piano. But you didn't think we were going to stop there, did you? We can make our website sound so much cooler with a bit more coding and the help of Web Audio API's sound styles to choose from.

Alex thinks we can take our sound options more toward Minecraft or whatever else we can dream up!

READY TO GO!

I. To add more options, **OPEN YOUR MUSIC.HTML FILE**. The Web Audio API has four different sound styles for us to choose from. To access them, we have to **ADD ONE MORE LINE** to our code:

```
var o = context.createOscillator()
var  g = context.createGain()
o.connect(g)
g.connect(context.destination)
o.type = 'triangle';
```

See the **"O.TYPE"** part? This is where we type **OUR SOUND STYLE**. You can try entering the following:

- **SINE:** This is the default sound type. When we first made our piano, it was using the "sine" style.

- **TRIANGLE:** This makes softer sounding notes, like a real piano would.

- **SQUARE:** This creates louder, brighter noises. It sounds almost like a doorbell!

- **SAWTOOTH:** This makes video game-style sounds, perfect for Minecraft!

2. Of course, all the best musicians play several notes at the same time. Can you think of a way we could do this? It's actually quite simple: We **COPY THE CODE ABOVE AND RENAME THE VARIABLES**:

```
var o = context.createOscillator()
var  g = context.createGain()
o.connect(g)
g.connect(context.destination)
o.type = 'sawtooth';

var o2 = context.createOscillator()
var  g2 = context.createGain()
o2.connect(g2)
g2.connect(context.destination)
o2.type = 'sawtooth';

o.start(0);
o2.start(0);

o.frequency.value = frequency;
o2.frequency.value = frequency;

var notelength = 5;

g.gain.exponentialRampToValueAtTime(0.00001, context.currentTime + notelength)
g2.gain.exponentialRampToValueAtTime(0.00001, context.currentTime + notelength)
```

3. Did you notice that we have copies of the *o* and *g* variables? We've named them *o2* and *g2*. At the moment, they're identical to the originals, so we can't hear any difference just yet.

So how do we **DECIDE WHAT THE SECOND NOTE SHOULD SOUND LIKE**? There are two ways: either by passing another value in when we run the function, or by changing the value somehow.

For instance, we could double the value for the second note like this (in JavaScript, the * symbol means "multiply by"):

```
o.frequency.value = frequency;
o2.frequency.value = frequency*2;
```

Or we could do this:

```
function playNote(frequency, frequency2){

        var o = context.createOscillator()
        var  g = context.createGain()
        o.connect(g)
        g.connect(context.destination)
        o.type = 'sawtooth';

        var o2 = context.createOscillator()
        var  g2 = context.createGain()
        o2.connect(g2)
        g2.connect(context.destination)
        o2.type = 'sawtooth';

        o.start(0);
        o2.start(0);

        o.frequency.value = frequency;
        o2.frequency.value = frequency2;
```

Of course, if we use this method, we also have to enter a second value when we run the function. This means that instead of doing this:

```
<img class = 'noteblock' onclick=playNote(195) src = 'note.jpg'/>
```

We'd do this:

```
<img class = 'noteblock' onclick=playNote(195,390) src = 'note.jpg'/>
```

We've definitely made our music even more interesting. But we can take it further with a little help from Scratch in Mission 3!

Mission 3

Audition a Band: Add Instruments with Scratch

If you're ready to create music that goes beyond our basic piano, we can do that! All it takes is a different coding tool to make what we need. There's a website called Scratch that lets us use building blocks to create simple programs. One of the great things about Scratch is that unlike the Web Audio API, it offers us lots of different instruments to play.

Just as more Minecraft characters are more fun, so are more instruments!

I. Open up your web browser and **GO TO HTTPS://SCRATCH.MIT.EDU**.

2. CLICK THE "CREATE" OPTION at the top of the screen. You'll be taken to the creation page. Do you see the "Scripts" section in the middle?

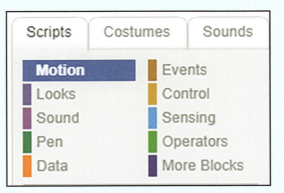

We'll be dragging blocks from here onto the blank space on the right. Each of these blocks represents a section of code: for instance, the "Repeat 10" block creates a loop where the *i* variable = 10.

3. In the scripts menu, click **EVENTS**. Now drag the **WHEN SPACE KEY IS PRESSED** block to the right. Under the **SOUNDS** tab, select the **PLAY DRUM I FOR 0.25 BEATS** block and connect it to the first one. Now press the spacebar and a drum will play! Cool, isn't it?

Let's make a constant drum beat. To do this, we'll need a loop that never ends. Click the **CONTROL TAB** and bring out a **FOREVER** block. By sticking this between the **WHEN SPACE KEY IS PRESSED** and **PLAY DRUM** blocks, we can start our drum line by pressing space. Try it now!

So far, so good! As far as drum lines go, though, it's pretty basic.

4. Why don't we add another drum in there? The bass drum is always a good place to start: **DRAG ANOTHER DRUM BLOCK** into the loop and click the drop-down menu to **SELECT THE BASS DRUM**.

Scratch Versus Javascript   X

There's one big difference between Scratch and JavaScript: Scratch lets you run two code blocks at the same time, but in JavaScript, things happen one after another. Notice how the bass drum isn't playing at the same time as the snare drum? That's because it comes after it in the loop.

To make noises happen at the same time, we have to create another loop. Grab another **WHEN SPACE KEY IS PRESSED** block and connect it to another **FOREVER** block. Now add a drum to this new loop. Try drum 6—the closed hi-hat, for instance. Now we're really starting to get somewhere!

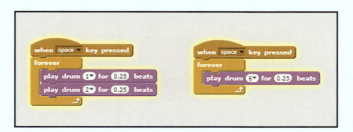

5. Here's the thing: Most songs have more than one instrument playing. Let's **ADD ANOTHER INSTRUMENT** and create a melody. We'll use the synth, since it's easy to stretch notes out for longer without the music sounding strange. **TRY MAKING THE FOLLOWING BLOCK, THEN PRESS THE SPACEBAR, FOLLOWED BY THE UP ARROW ON YOUR KEYBOARD.**

If you timed it right, the synth should be playing in time with the drums!

6. We'll **ADD ANOTHER INSTRUMENT** for extra flair. There's one difference this time, though: we won't be putting it on a loop, so you'll be responsible for pressing the right key at the right time!

```
when down arrow ▼ key pressed
set instrument to 16▼
play note 72▼ for 0.5 beats
play note 69▼ for 0.3 beats
play note 67▼ for 0.4 beats
play note 60▼ for 0.5 beats
play note 60▼ for 0.5 beats
```

Try playing this section during the last synth note. Sounds good, doesn't it?

7. Why don't we add **ONE LAST INSTRUMENT**?

```
when right arrow ▼ key pressed
set instrument to 6▼
play note 48▼ for 0.1 beats
play note 55▼ for 0.1 beats
play note 57▼ for 0.3 beats
play note 55▼ for 0.1 beats
play note 53▼ for 0.1 beats
play note 55▼ for 0.2 beats
play note 48▼ for 0.3 beats
play note 48▼ for 0.5 beats
play note 72▼ for 0.3 beats
play note 69▼ for 0.1 beats
play note 67▼ for 0.3 beats
```

Okay, you know how we played the last part at the end of the synth section? From now on, let's play the vibraphone on the first synth section, the bass on the second, and repeat. That sounds great—well done!

Why don't you try switching up some of the instruments now? You can also change the beats value in order to make certain sounds play for longer. Remember, the lower the value in the beats section, the shorter the note. Use this playing time as your warmup before we create your own Minecraft music in Mission 4!

8. Before you leave the page, make sure all your work doesn't disappear! Download your work by clicking the **FILE TAB AND CHOOSING "DOWNLOAD TO YOUR COMPUTER."** To get your program back in the future, just click **"UPLOAD FROM YOUR COMPUTER"** and double-click your program file.

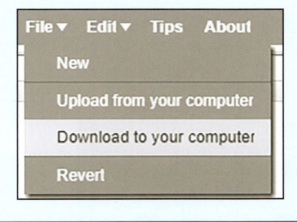

MISSION 4

SUPER SOUNDTRACK: CREATE YOUR OWN MINECRAFT SONGS

As a fan of the game, you know that Minecraft has a very specific musical style. The songs you hear when playing are usually fairly slow, with long piano notes and maybe a little synth in the background. So let's make our own music that sounds as though it belongs in the game!

If you can hear it in your head, you can create it through coding!

READY TO GO!

1. We'll begin by heading back to Scratch (**HTTPS://SCRATCH.MIT.EDU**). Start a new project by clicking the **CREATE BUTTON** at the top of the page.

2. This time, we're going to **MAKE IT EASIER TO PLAY MULTIPLE SOUNDS AT ONCE**. If you create several different blocks of code and use the same button to start them, everything works perfectly! See for yourself:

```
when  left arrow ▾  key pressed          when  left arrow ▾  key pressed
forever                                   forever
    set instrument to 21▾                     set instrument to 21▾
    play note 62▾ for 6 beats                 play note 53▾ for 6 beats
    play note 65▾ for 6 beats                 play note 60▾ for 6 beats
    play note 67▾ for 8 beats                 play note 57▾ for 8 beats
```

3. Our setup creates some nice synth chords when the left arrow key is pressed. But Minecraft music usually starts with piano first, so let's **MAKE A CALM TUNE**:

```
when  space ▾  key pressed
forever
    set instrument to 2▾
    play note 74▾ for 3 beats
    play note 69▾ for 2 beats
    play note 67▾ for 2 beats
    play note 65▾ for 0.3 beats
    play note 69▾ for 0.3 beats
    play note 65▾ for 0.3 beats
    play note 74▾ for 2 beats
    play note 69▾ for 2 beats
    play note 67▾ for 2 beats
```

4. Have you noticed the problem yet? If multiple instruments try to play a note at the same time, Scratch gets confused and plays every note with the same instrument. To stop this happening, we need to **TELL OUR DIFFERENT MUSICAL PARTS TO WAIT FOR EACH OTHER TO FINISH**.

To do this, count the total number of beats in each part. Our piano piece has 13.9 beats and our synth parts each have 20 beats. One beat is equal to one second, so we need to tell each part to wait a certain number of seconds. Luckily, there's a block that does just that.

Drag the **WAIT** block to the bottom of each loop. In the piano wait box, type 20. In the synth boxes, type 13.9. Now try playing the song again—everything should play exactly as we expected!

```
when space ▼ key pressed
forever
    set instrument to 2 ▼
    play note 74 ▼ for 3 beats
    play note 69 ▼ for 2 beats
    play note 67 ▼ for 2 beats
    play note 65 ▼ for 0.3 beats
    play note 69 ▼ for 0.3 beats
    play note 65 ▼ for 0.3 beats
    play note 74 ▼ for 2 beats
    play note 69 ▼ for 2 beats
    play note 67 ▼ for 2 beats
    wait 20 secs
```

```
when left arrow ▼ key pressed
forever
    set instrument to 21 ▼
    play note 62 ▼ for 6 beats
    play note 55 ▼ for 6 beats
    play note 67 ▼ for 8 beats
    wait 13.9 secs
```

```
when left arrow ▼ key pressed
forever
    set instrument to 21 ▼
    play note 53 ▼ for 6 beats
    play note 60 ▼ for 6 beats
    play note 57 ▼ for 8 beats
    wait 13.9 secs
```

STRANGE SOUNDS   X

You might have noticed something strange in this section. Scratch's note selector only goes up to 72, but we have several notes that are higher than that. You can actually type in any number you like, but **most notes over 100 are uncomfortable to hear**, so it's a good idea to avoid those.

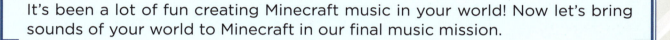

It's been a lot of fun creating Minecraft music in your world! Now let's bring sounds of your world to Minecraft in our final music mission.

Mission 5

Clash of the Worlds: Bring Your Sounds to Minecraft

For our final music mission, we're going to record a sound and put it into the game of Minecraft! First, you'll need a way to record your sound. You can use a microphone or cell phone, or just find a sound online that you'd like to use. The next step is to decide what kind of Minecraft sound you want to replace. Then we're set to code and make it happen!

You can make any sound swaps you like— from changing the background music to the noise a pig makes. Nothing is off limits!

LET'S GET SET

I. Once you've made a decision, go ahead and **RECORD YOUR SOUND**. Unless you're recording music, make sure your sound is only a few seconds long. If it's too long, it might not work properly. Once you're done, **SAVE THE FILE IN THE .OGG FORMAT**. This is very important since it's the only format that will work.

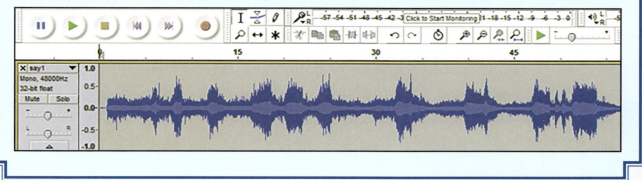

READY TO GO!

1. So how do we get our sound into the game? We're going to **CREATE A RESOURCE PACK**. This step lets us add our own sounds (and images) without deleting the original ones. First, we need to **FIND MINECRAFT'S RESOURCE PACK FOLDER**.

Username ▸ AppData ▸ Roaming ▸ .minecraft ▸			
Name	Date modified	Type	Size
asm	30/09/2015 10:56	File folder	
assets	27/03/2018 16:52	File folder	
config	04/10/2015 10:31	File folder	
crash-reports	04/10/2015 16:35	File folder	
journeymap	04/10/2015 16:35	File folder	
libraries	06/09/2016 21:00	File folder	
logs	05/04/2018 10:05	File folder	
minecraft launcher	29/09/2015 17:54	File folder	
mods	06/09/2016 21:42	File folder	
resourcepacks	05/04/2018 09:37	File folder	
resources	06/09/2016 21:37	File folder	
saves	05/04/2018 10:09	File folder	
server-resource-packs	06/09/2016 21:09	File folder	
shaderpacks	30/09/2015 10:08	File folder	
stats	06/09/2016 21:37	File folder	
TEST	27/03/2018 16:50	File folder	
texturepacks	08/10/2015 12:54	File folder	
texturepacks-mp-cache	08/10/2015 12:54	File folder	
versions	27/03/2018 17:05	File folder	
launcher_log	05/04/2018 10:13	Text Document	564 KB

IF YOU'RE USING A WINDOWS COMPUTER, press the Windows key, then type the following into the search box, replacing [YOUR_USERNAME] with your actual username:
C:\Users\[YOUR_USERNAME]\AppData\Roaming\.minecraft\resourcepacks

IF YOU'RE USING A MAC COMPUTER, click the Go to Folder option in the menu and type this:
~/Library/Application Support/minecraft/resourcepacks

The resource pack folder should open.

2. CREATE A NEW FOLDER inside the resource pack folder. You can name it whatever you like, but in this case, we'll call it **"SOUND PACK"**. Inside, we need to create a new file, so open up your TextEditor and save the file as **"PACK.MCMETA"**.

Copy and paste the following code into the pack.mcmeta file:

```
{
    "pack": {
        "pack_format": 3,
        "description": "Coding for Minecrafters Sound Pack"
    }
}
```

Here's where it gets tricky: the number after the "pack_format" part should be different based on the version of Minecraft you're running.

To find out which version of Minecraft you have, open the program and log in. You'll see a version number on the **PLAY** button. Here are the correct "pack_format" numbers for each version:

Version Number	"pack_format" number
Version 1.6, 1.7, or 1.8	1
Version 1.9 or 1.10	2
Version 1.11 or 1.12	3
Version 1.13	4

We're using Minecraft version 1.12.2, so our "pack_format" number should be "3". Once you've entered the correct number, save the file and close it.

3. Inside your **SOUND PACK** folder, create another folder called **"ASSETS"**. Inside that folder, create one called **"MINECRAFT"**. Inside *that* folder, create a folder called **"SOUNDS"**.

Username ▸ AppData ▸ Roaming ▸ .minecraft ▸ resourcepacks ▸ Sound pack ▸ assets ▸ minecraft ▸ sounds ▸

We're taking this step because Minecraft is really strict about where sounds and images go and what they're called. Now we've hit a problem: we don't know the name of the file we're trying to replace. So how do we find this out?

4. To begin with, **GO BACK TO THE ".MINECRAFT" FOLDER**. You should be able to do this by clicking the address bar at the top of your screen.

Next, enter the folder called **"ASSETS"**. Go into the **"INDEXES"** folder and open the file with the version number you're using. Let's say we wanted to replace the noise that chickens make when they're walking around. We'd press the **CONTROL BUTTON AND F KEY** at the same time, then type "chicken".

You'll see the names of several chicken sound files. The one we're looking for is "say1.ogg". From the results, we can see that our replacement audio file should be placed inside a specific series of folders. We'll have to create these folders in our resource pack in order for our new sound to work.

```
"minecraft/sounds/mob/chicken/say1.ogg": {
  "hash": "74e5422bd83bb2041a6f0d09644bc095c0e9e21a",
  "size": 7956
},
```

5. Go back to your resource pack, and go into the "sounds" folder we created earlier. Now create a folder called "mob" and inside it, another folder called "chicken". Place your sound file into the "chicken" folder and rename it **"SAY1.OGG"**.

6. Okay, it's time to see if our resource pack works! Open Minecraft and on the main screen, click **OPTIONS**. In the options menu, click on **RESOURCE PACKS**.

If everything has worked as planned, you'll see your resource pack in the left box. Hover the mouse pointer over it and click the arrow that appears to load it into our game. Now click the **DONE** button, and the **DONE** button on the next page to return to the menu.

7. Here's the thing: We can't just run around hoping to find a chicken, so we'll use a Creative mode world to see if our new sound has loaded properly. Click **SINGLEPLAYER** on the menu, then **CREATE NEW WORLD**, then click the **GAME MODE** box twice to set it to creative. When you're ready, click **CREATE NEW WORLD** again.

Once the game loads, get yourself to an open stretch of land. Then, hit the **E KEY** and click the **MISCELLANEOUS TAB**. Scroll down until you find the **CHICKEN EGG** item. Drag this item to your toolbar. Finally, press **E** again. Now we can test our sound pack out!

Click the right mouse button to spawn a chicken. It should now play the sound you recorded earlier! Don't worry if the game freezes for a second or two; this is normal and only happens the first time the sound is played. Congratulations, you've just modded Minecraft!

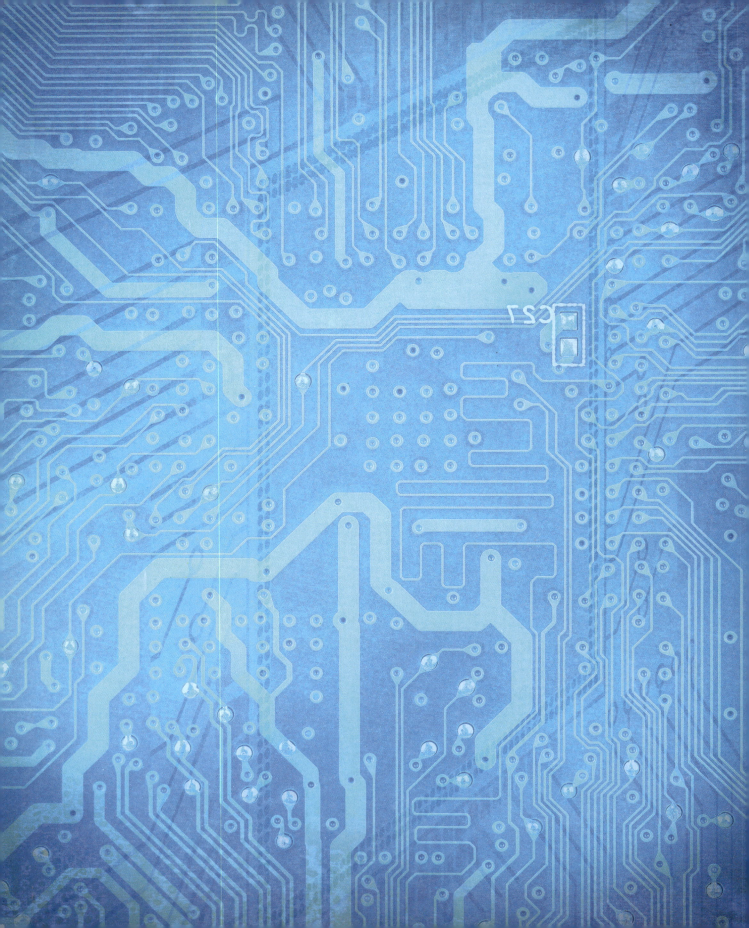

GREAT GAMING

Mission 1

Minecraft Maze: Create a Basic Game in Scratch

Creating a game can be simple when you break down the steps. In order to build a game, we need three things: a way for the player to interact with the objects on the screen, a goal, and some obstacles. The goal can be anything from reaching a certain area to scoring a certain number of points. The obstacles might be monsters, puzzles, or even walls. Let's get gaming by creating a maze!

Have dreams of becoming a game designer?
See how coding can put you on the right track!

READY TO GO!

I. Start by going to Scratch at **HTTPS://SCRATCH.MIT.EDU**, then click the **CREATE** button at the top of the screen.

2. The first thing we need to do is **CREATE A SPRITE**. Sprites are just what we call the pictures of the game's characters and objects. There's a big picture of a cat on the left-hand side, for instance—that's a sprite.

Right-click the small picture of the cat and delete it. In the bar above, you'll see a **PAINTBRUSH ICON**. Click this to start drawing your own sprites.

We'll start by **DRAWING A BOAT**. Now, it's very important the boat is drawn facing the right-hand side. Otherwise, it'll move in a strange way later on. Use the tools on the left to draw a rectangle, then add two lines to make a pointy front part. When you're done, your boat should look something like this:

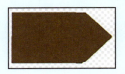

Now drag your boat into the center of the drawing area. Great work!

3. If you click the **SCRIPTS TAB** at the top of the screen, you can begin adding some controls. See if you can create the code blocks below. What happens if you push the arrow keys? That's right, your boat should turn and move!

```
when up arrow key pressed          when right arrow key pressed
point in direction 0               point in direction 90
move 10 steps                      move 10 steps


when down arrow key pressed         when left arrow key pressed
point in direction 180             point in direction -90
move 10 steps                      move 10 steps
```

This works by turning the boat 90° depending on the direction you choose. To turn left, we move -90°, to turn right, it's 90°, and to face the opposite direction, it's 180°.

There is one small issue, though. Our boat is too big. Try shrinking it to a better size by clicking it and using the **SHRINK** button in the top bar.

4. Next, we'll **MAKE THE WALLS** of our maze. Create a new sprite and draw a green rectangle standing on its end. You'll also have to do create another sprite that's exactly the same, but lying on its side.

You can drag these into the window on the left and shrink them until they're the right size. Try right-clicking them and selecting **DUPLICATE** from the list. See how a copy appears? Drag these copies around the window on the left to make your maze!

5. Finally, **CREATE ONE LAST SPRITE**. This will be our goal. Let's say Steve is trying to sail home before it gets dark—the goal should really be a house, right? Draw a house, shrink it down, and place it at the end of your maze.

6. The next step is to **ADD LOGIC** to our game. What does this mean? Well, logic is what we call the code that tells the game what the rules are. For instance, we need to add logic to prevent the boat from being able to sail right over our green walls!

To do this, we need to add a small block of code to each of our movement blocks. Note that this will only work if all your walls are the same color:

```
when  up arrow  ▼  key pressed
point in direction  0 ▼
move  10  steps
if        touching color  ▢  ?      then
    set x to  -130
    set y to  -150
```

```
when  right arrow  ▼  key pressed
point in direction  90 ▼
move  10  steps
if        touching color  ▢  ?      then
    set x to  -130
    set y to  -150
```

```
when  down arrow  ▼  key pressed
point in direction  180 ▼
move  10  steps
if        touching color  ▢  ?      then
    set x to  -130
    set y to  -150
```

```
when  left arrow  ▼  key pressed
point in direction  -90 ▼
move  10  steps
if        touching color  ▢  ?      then
    set x to  -130
    set y to  -150
```

This code tells the game that if you touch the walls (which are green), you have to go straight back to the start! Now, depending on the layout of your maze, you might end up somewhere different. In this case, try changing the **SET X TO** and **SET Y TO** values. The X value tells the boat how far to move to the right, and the Y value is for moving it to the bottom of the screen.

7. There's one last thing to do. We need to make something happen when Steve reaches his house. In our maze, it's impossible to finish the maze by pressing up, left, or down, so we only need to add the following code to the

WHEN RIGHT ARROW KEY IS PRESSED block. You might have to add it to every movement block, though, depending on your maze.

You should also note that if you have lots of walls, Steve's house might not be called Sprite13. In this case, check the window under the game itself to find the right sprite number. Next, change the code block to use the correct sprite. Okay, so let's see what happens when we finish the maze....

Looking good! There are a few final tweaks to make.

8. You'll notice that the game doesn't end and you can still move around, so let's fix that. We just have to **CHANGE THE MOVEMENT CODE BLOCK** a little:

```
when right arrow ▼ key pressed
point in direction 90▼
move 10 steps
if      touching color ■ ?   then
    set x to -130
    set y to -150

if      touching Sprite13 ▼ ?   then
    say You win! for 2 secs
    hide
```

Now the boat will disappear two seconds after touching the house, as if Steve has gone inside. Nicely done! You can restart the game by clicking the red stop sign above the game window:

```
Untitled                                    ⚑  ●
```

You can also **ENTER A NAME FOR YOUR GAME** by typing into the box on the left, if you'd like.

9. The last problem is that our water is white! To change this, click the **PAINTBRUSH ICON** on the left-hand side of the sprite menu.

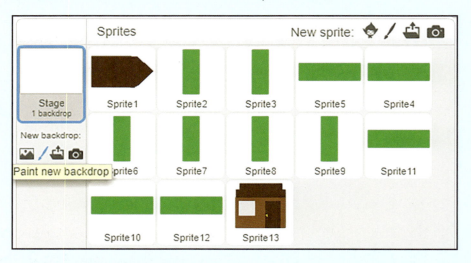

Now **FILL THE ENTIRE BACKDROP** with a nice blue color. There you go, instant water!

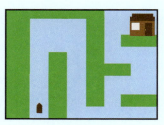

10. Make sure to click the **FILE TAB** at the top of the screen and hit **"DOWNLOAD TO YOUR COMPUTER"** so you can show your game to your friends later!

Congratulations on building a maze with Scratch! For Mission 2, what about building a game that lets you build?

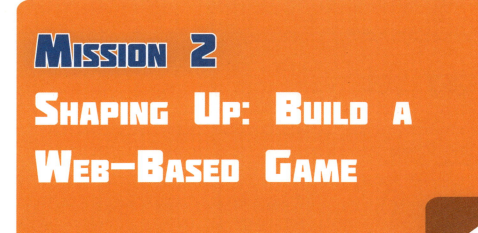

MISSION 2

SHAPING UP: BUILD A WEB-BASED GAME

You can create games that work through websites. You got a taste with the storytelling adventure game we created for Steve back in Web Design (page 27). But we can take the coding to a more advanced level to create even more functionality. Let's help Steve add a building game to his website!

Blocks are an essential part of building in Minecraft.
What shapes can you add to gaming?

LET'S GET SET

I. Let's return to the website we built for Steve. Start by adding the following line to your **INDEX.HTML** page:

```
<button id="mainbutton" onclick="location.href='games.html';">Play a Game</button>
```

2. Now we need to create a page called **"GAMES.HTML"**. Make sure to save it in the same place as all your other HTML pages, then copy the following code into it:

```
<!DOCTYPE html>
<html>

<head>

</head>

<body>

</body>
<script>

</script>

</html>
```

3. In the <head> section, **ADD LINKS TO OUR CSS AND JQUERY FILES**:

```
<script src="https://ajax.googleapis.com/ajax/libs/jquery/3.3.1/jquery.min.js"></script>
<script src="https://ajax.googleapis.com/ajax/libs/jqueryui/1.12.1/jquery-ui.min.js"></script>
<link rel="stylesheet" type="text/css" href="style.css">
```

4. Finally, **ADD A BUTTON** to the <body>:

```
<button id="mainbutton">Create shape</button>
```

So far, our page is pretty boring. That button is interesting, though, isn't it?

Create shape

READY TO GO!

5. We're going to **CREATE A FUNCTION THAT RANDOMLY GENERATES DIFFERENT SIZES OF SQUARES**. In the <script> tags at the bottom of our page, add the following:

```
function createShape(){

    shapeCount = shapeCount+1;

}
```

Understand it so far? Whenever we click the button, the *shapeCount* variable increases by one. We'll use this to keep track of how many shapes there are, and apply different effects to each shape.

6. Let's find a way to **RANDOMLY CHOOSE A SIZE AND COLOR FOR OUR SHAPES**. We've already seen "Math.floor" way back in the design chapter (page 25), but notice how our "Math.random" has numbers after it? These tell it to create a random whole number (not a decimal) with a minimum size of five pixels and a maximum of 100 pixels.

```
function createShape(){

    shapeCount = shapeCount+1;

    var size = Math.floor((Math.random()*100)+5)
    var colors = ["red","green", "blue"];
    var randomColor = colors[Math.floor(Math.random()*colors.length)];

}
```

The bottom line here chooses a random color from our colors array. Feel free to add more if you like!

Here's the tricky bit: we need to **GIVE EACH SHAPE A UNIQUE ID**. To do this, we'll use the following line of code:

```
var shapeID = 'shape'+shapeCount;
```

It creates a new variable called *shapeID* and sets it to the word "shape" followed by our current *shapeCount*. Now the first shape will have an ID of "shape1", our second will be "shape2", and so on.

7. Next, we tell our function to **ADD A NEW <DIV> TO THE PAGE** and give it the latest shape ID. The position of the different quotation marks is very important here; the double quotation marks (" ") close text and allow us to enter variables, but the single marks (' ') are so the HTML knows what the ID is.

```
$('body').append("<div id = '"+shapeID+"' ></div>");
```

8. Did you know that we can change CSS properties using jQuery? This saves us from having to create a specific CSS section for every possible shape. Let's **ADD A RANDOM HEIGHT, WIDTH, AND COLOR TO OUR SHAPES**:

```
$('#'+shapeID).css("width", size+"px");
$('#'+shapeID).css("min-height", size+"px");
$('#'+shapeID).css("background-color", randomColor);
```

This is interesting. See how we've used a variable in our jQuery selector? If we'd typed "#shapeID", it wouldn't have worked, since none of our elements have that ID. This code tells jQuery to look for elements with the ID of "shape1", "shape2", and so on.

9. Finally, let's **MAKE OUR SHAPES DRAGGABLE**.

```
$('#'+shapeID).draggable();
```

10. Now **SAVE EVERYTHING AND RELOAD** the page. What happens when you click the button?

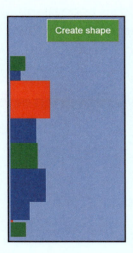

We get a selection of random squares. These can be dragged around to build houses, cars, or really, anything you like!

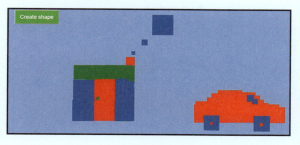

This functionality is pretty good, but it can be annoying to scroll all the way down to grab the block you want.

II. Now, create a class so we can **CHANGE WHERE THE BLOCKS APPEAR**. In your CSS file, type this:

```css
.block{

    float:right;
    margin: 3px 3px 3px 3px;
    display: inline-block;


}
```

Our blocks should start appearing at the right-hand side of the screen, and show up in a neat row. We've also added a little space around each block so that it's easier to grab the one you want.

I2. So far, we've made a pretty cool building game! We can **MAKE IT EVEN BETTER WITH A FEW EXTRA LINES OF CODE**, though. At the very bottom of your function, add this:

```javascript
var circle = Math.floor((Math.random()*10)+1);

if(circle > 7){
    $('#'+shapeID).css("border-radius", "50px");
}
```

Every time we create a shape, the variable *circle* chooses a number between 1 and 10. If the *circle* variable is greater than 7, we round the shapes edges out and it becomes a circle! In other words, we have about a 20% chance of creating a circle whenever we click the button.

Let's take a look:

Yup, when we generate 20 shapes, we get four circles. That's 1 in 5 shapes, or 20%. This tells us that our IF statement is working properly. Nice work!

You can change the probability of getting a circle by making the number in the IF statement lower or higher. Try experimenting with what you've created! In the next gaming mission, we'll be keeping score.

MISSION 3
SCORE AGAINST CREEPERS: CODE A GAME WITH A SCOREBOARD

Mazes and building games are lots of fun. But if your idea of a game comes with a high score as a goal, this mission might be just what you've been waiting to create. Let's see how all of our coding knowledge can add up!

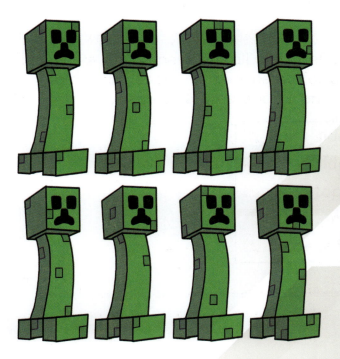

Your coding knowledge can help you create a creeper battle and keep score for the victory!

LET'S GET SET

1. We're going to need the entire screen for this game, so we can't put it on the "games.html" page we made earlier. With that in mind, we'll **CREATE A NEW PAGE CALLED "GAMES2.HTML".** Feel free to add a link to it on the "index.html" page if you like.

2. Let's **SET UP OUR PAGE**. This should be feeling pretty familiar to you at this point. Think you can do it without looking at the code below? Give it a shot.

```html
<!DOCTYPE html>
<html>

<head>
    <script src="https://ajax.googleapis.com/ajax/libs/jquery/3.3.1/jquery.min.js"></script>
    <link rel="stylesheet" type="text/css" href="style.css">
</head>

<body>

</body>

<script>

</script>

</html>
```

3. Inside our <body>, we're going to add something different for this game. We need a **PLACE TO PUT THE USER'S CURRENT SCORE**, the highest score they've gotten, and how much time is left.

```html
<button id = "mainbutton" class = "gameinfo" onclick = startGame() >Start!</button>
<p id = 'timer' class = 'gameinfo'></p>
<p id = 'scoreboard' class = 'gameinfo'></p>
<p id = 'highscore' class = 'gameinfo'></p>

<div id = 'gamearea'></div>
```

4. Next is the **<SCRIPT> TAGS**. The first thing to do is make sure you can't click the start button more than once. This would cause all kinds of problems! We'll put this code into a new **FUNCTION CALLED "STARTGAME"**:

```javascript
function startGame(){

    document.getElementById("mainbutton").disabled = true;
    $('#mainbutton').css("background-color", "grey");

}
```

SAVE YOUR PAGE and try clicking the button. What happens?

The button changes color, but it also stops you from clicking it again. Good work! We're now well on our way to having a fully functional game!

READY TO GO!

5. Now let's **ADD SOME VARIABLES** for our game:

```
var highscore = 0;

function startGame(){

    document.getElementById("mainbutton").disabled = true;
    $('#mainbutton').css("background-color", "grey");

    var gameLength = 60;
    var monsterCount = 0;
    var score = 0;

}
```

Notice how the *highscore* **VARIABLE** is outside of our function. This means it will be set to 0 when the page loads, but never again. If it was inside our function, the *highscore* would be lost whenever a new game was started.

6. We're going to **ADD A TIME LIMIT** to our game. That's what the *gameLength* **VARIABLE** controls. See how it's set to 60? That means our game will run for 60 seconds. To time events in JavaScript, we use the setInterval function, like so:

```
var round = setInterval(function() {
        gameLength = gameLength - 1;

        document.getElementById("timer").innerHTML = gameLength+" seconds left";
        document.getElementById("scoreboard").innerHTML = "Your score: "+score ;
        document.getElementById("highscore").innerHTML = "High score: "+highscore ;
},1000)
```

That number in brackets tells the function how often to run the code above. Here, it's 1000. This is in milliseconds, so 1000 means the code will run once every second. What does our code actually do? Well, it takes one second off of the remaining game time and displays it in the timer <div>. It also keeps track of the current score and high scores, but we'll add that code a little later.

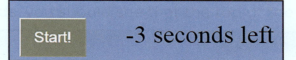

Try clicking the button and waiting until the game runs out of time. Can you see the problem?

Wait, that doesn't look right! We need to **TELL THE CODE TO STOP COUNTING** when the remaining time equals zero. We also need to make that button clickable again! Luckily, this is easily done with an IF statement.

```
if(gameLength > 0){

    gameLength = gameLength - 1;

    document.getElementById("timer").innerHTML = gameLength+" seconds left";
    document.getElementById("scoreboard").innerHTML = "Your score: "+score ;
    document.getElementById("highscore").innerHTML = "High score: "+highscore ;

}else{

    document.getElementById("mainbutton").disabled = false;
    $('#mainbutton').css("background-color", "");
    clearInterval(round);

}
```

Here, it says that if there's at least one second left, keep updating the timer and scores. If you're out of time, our code will make the button clickable and use the clearInterval function to stop our timer completely. If you reload the page and try clicking the button, the timer should stop at zero now. Better yet, this will work every time the button is pressed.

7. Now that we know how to time events, let's go ahead and **CREATE ANOTHER SETINTERVAL FUNCTION** with a two-second timer. While we're at it, why not add an IF statement just like the one we used above:

```
var game = setInterval(function() {

    if(gameLength>0){

    }else{

    clearInterval(game);

    }
}, 2000)
```

8. Here's where things get a bit more difficult. We're going to **CREATE A NEW MONSTER** every two seconds. To do this, we'll assign each monster a different ID, just like we did with the blocks in Great Gaming Mission 2. Can you remember how to do this? Don't worry if you can't—go ahead and enter the code below into the top part of the IF statement, inside the brackets and before the ELSE part:

```
monsterCount = monsterCount+1;
monsterID = "monster"+monsterCount;
$('#gamearea').append("<img src = 'creeper.jpg' id = '"+monsterCount+"'/>")
```

So every two seconds, we add one to the *monsterCount* **VARIABLE**. Next, we turn that into a usable ID by adding the word "monster" to the front. For instance, "monster1", "monster2", and "monster3". The last line here adds the creeper image to the page and gives it this unique ID.

9. The goal of this game is to get points by clicking creepers. The creepers should then disappear. We can **GET RID OF THEM BY USING A LITTLE BIT OF JQUERY**:

```
$('#'+monsterCount).click(function(){

    $('#'+monsterCount).remove();
    score = score+10;

})
```

Now when you click a creeper, it disappears and your score goes up by ten points. There are a couple of problems though: the creepers always appear in the same place, and if you don't click them, more appear.

10. To **MAKE THE CREEPERS APPEAR IN RANDOM PLACES**, we'll add two lines of code; one gets the X value (how far to the right the creeper is) and one gets the Y value (how far from the top of the screen the creeper is). It works like drawing a graph! Add this code underneath where you create the *monsterID* variable:

```
monsterX   = Math.floor((Math.random()*80)+1);
monsterY   = Math.floor((Math.random()*20)+1);
```

Try changing these numbers if the creeper goes off the side of the screen. One set of numbers may not work perfectly for every different computer monitor.

11. See the line where we add the creeper image? Just underneath it, **ADD THIS CODE**:

```
$('#'+monsterCount).css("margin-left", monsterX+"%");
$('#'+monsterCount).css("margin-top", monsterY+"%");
$('#'+monsterCount).css("width", "8%");
```

Notice how we're moving the creeper away from the top and left-hand sides of the screen using percentages instead of specific values. This means our game will even be playable on smaller screens. We've also reduced its size a little, to make it harder to click on.

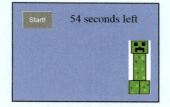

12. Okay, let's **MAKE THESE CREEPERS DISAPPEAR** after two seconds if they aren't clicked. All we need to do is delete any creepers that are around before anything else happens. Go to your second setInterval section. Inside your *gameLength* IF statement, make the following code the first line:

```
$('#'+monsterCount).remove();
```

You should also add this line at the bottom of your ELSE statement so that the creeper disappears when the game ends.

YOUR GAME, YOUR CODE   X

As always, feel free to change anything you like.

• Want to click chickens instead of creepers? Just change the image.

• Want to get more points, give yourself more time, or change the creeper's size? It's as simple as changing the variable values.

• Is the game too easy or too hard? In this case, you might want to change how often your second setInterval function runs. Remember, this is the value at the very end, inside the brackets. If you really want a challenge, try using a value of 500! Anything lower than that will probably be too hard, though.

13. SAVE YOUR PAGE and reload it. Your game is working *almost* perfectly. Can you see what's wrong with the image below?

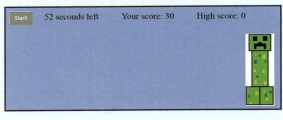

Our high score isn't working! There's no need to panic—this is the easiest part! You know the function that says what to do when a monster is clicked? Go ahead and change its code to this:

```
$('#'+monsterCount).click(function(){

    $('#'+monsterCount).remove();
    score = score+10;

    if(score>highscore){
        highscore = score;
    }

})
```

Now whenever you increase your score, the game checks to see if you've beaten the high score. If so, it'll update the high-score box at the top of the screen.

Your score: 30   High score: 30

Congratulations, you've just created your first competitive game! But don't get too tied up trying to beat your high score. We still have two gaming missions remaining for you.

BEATING THE BUGS

Coding and debugging go hand in hand. Let's see if there are any bugs left in this game. Try the following and think about what should happen in each case:

- Set a high score then beat it in your next game.

- Set a high score and don't beat it in your next game.

- See if you can cheat by clicking a creeper twice.

- See if you can cheat by changing the amount of points you get. (This doesn't work—why not?)

MISSION 4
THE NEXT LEVEL: ADVANCE YOUR CODING GAME

When you first picked up this book, you probably didn't know much about code, but now you're coding incredible creations! We built a really impressive game in the last mission, and you should be proud of yourself for your coding achievement. But you know that game programmers can't go long without wanting an update, with new amazing features. So we're going to add a few tweaks to the game we just built in order to make it more difficult, but also more fun.

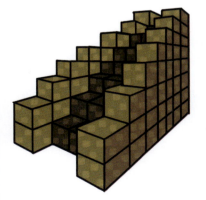

The heart of true programmers is never quite satisfied! Once the coding is in place and working, they're already thinking up the next update.

LET'S GET SET

1. Pretend you've built a chicken farm in Minecraft. Everything is going well until suddenly you hear a hissing sound and realize that some creepers have gotten into it! The aim of our game is going to be to click *only* the creepers. It's harder than it sounds because chickens will also be popping up and if you click one of those, you'll lose points! To make things even more difficult, sometimes the images will be smaller than usual.

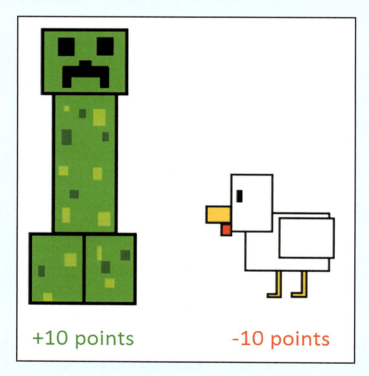

+10 points   -10 points

2. Open your games2.html file for tweaking.

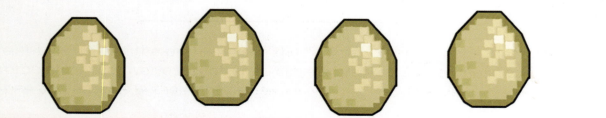

READY TO GO!

3. Let's start by changing the size of the monsters randomly. To do this, we'll **CREATE A NEW VARIABLE NAMED** *monsterSize*. This randomly chooses a width between 3% and 12% for our creepers. Put this underneath the *monsterX* and *monsterY* lines. Bear in mind that you can change these numbers if the images show up too big or too small:

```
monstersize  = Math.floor((Math.random()*12)+3);
```

Now we have to actually **SET THE MONSTER'S WIDTH**. Put this line underneath the one where we change its position:

```
$('#'+monsterCount).css("width", monstersize+"%");
```

When you **SAVE AND RELOAD THE PAGE**, the creeper should change size. Let's see if it works....

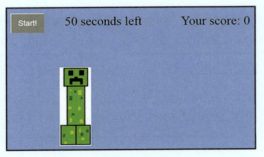

4. Next, let's **MAKE CHICKENS APPEAR RANDOMLY**. We'll create a function to get a random number between 1 and 10. If the number is greater than 5, we'll make a creeper pop up. If not, it'll be a chicken instead.

```
function chooseCreature(monsterCount){

    var creature  = Math.floor((Math.random() * 10)+1);

    if(creature >5){

        $('#gamearea').append("<img src = 'creeper.jpg' class = 'creeper' id = '"+monsterCount+"'/>")

    }else{

        $('#gamearea').append("<img src = 'chicken.jpg' class = 'chicken' id = '"+monsterCount+"'/>")

    }
}
```

Notice how we've added classes to these images, even though we aren't using the CSS file to change how they look? This is so we can tell jQuery what to do when specific images are clicked—normally we'd use the ID, but we've already used that to get rid of creepers when they're clicked.

5. We have our function ready to go, so now it's only a matter of **TELLING OUR PAGE WHEN TO RUN IT**. The **SECOND SETINTERVAL SECTION** is in charge of spawning elements, so let's put it in there. We'll place this next line of code just underneath the *monsterSize* line we added a moment ago.

```
chooseCreature(monsterCount)
```

SAVE AND RELOAD YOUR PAGE. If everything's working as intended, you should see chickens appear every now and then.

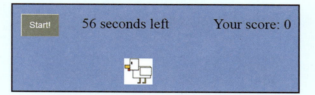

6. We're making good progress. However, nothing happens when you click the chicken. This is because we haven't added the right code yet. Take a look through your HTML page until you **FIND THE PART THAT DOES SOMETHING WHEN A CREEPER IS CLICKED**. After this, we're going to add an almost identical function:

```
$('.chicken').click(function(){

    $('#'+monsterCount).remove();
    score = score-10;

})
```

It's pretty simple, right? We've made it so that clicking a chicken reduces the score by ten points. We've left out the high score part, since it's not possible to get a new high score by clicking chickens. After all, you'd actually be lowering your score! **MAKE SURE IT WORKS BY CLICKING A CHICKEN:**

Your score: -10

7. Now the only issue with our game is that there's no feedback other than the scoreboard. In other words, new players wouldn't know that clicking a chicken was wrong unless they checked their score.

What happens in a game if you try something you're not supposed to? Often, an object will shake or bounce to show you that you can't do a certain thing. **LET'S TRY MAKING OUR CHICKEN BOUNCE WHEN CLICKED.**

If you think back to our animation missions, you'll know that **WE NEED THE JQUERY UI PLUGIN** for this. Inside your document's <head> section, add the links to jQuery UI:

```
<link rel="stylesheet" href="https://ajax.googleapis.com/ajax/libs/jqueryui/1.12.1/themes/smoothness/jquery-ui.css">
<script src="https://ajax.googleapis.com/ajax/libs/jqueryui/1.12.1/jquery-ui.min.js"></script>
```

Move down the page until you reach the creeper and chicken ".click" sections. Inside the chicken's function, change the line with ".remove()" so that it says this:

```
$('#'+monsterCount).effect( "bounce", "slow" )
```

8. As for the creeper, you can use whichever effect you like best. The "pulsate" effect looks particularly good since it makes the creeper flash, just like in Minecraft. **TRY ADDING THE PULSATE EFFECT** with the code below:

```
$('#'+monsterCount).effect("pulsate",  "slow");
```

9. But wait! Since we're not removing the creeper immediately anymore, you can click each monster lots of times to rack up loads of points! That's obviously not fair, so how can we fix this?

jQuery has a nice feature that **MAKES IT SO THAT AN ELEMENT CAN ONLY BE CLICKED ONCE.** Without it, we'd need to create a variable to check if the monster had been clicked, then reset this variable whenever a new creeper appeared. Instead, we can do this with a single line of code. So go ahead and replace the first line of the creeper's ".click()" script with this:

```
$('.creeper').one('click', function() {
```

If you like, you can do the same for the chicken. This isn't necessary, though, because if you click a chicken lots of times, it doesn't give you any kind of advantage.

| Start! | 54 seconds left | Your score: 20 | High score: 60 |

Keep Going   X

Well done on these game tweaks! However, **if you want to keep going, you can add or change all kinds of elements.** Some coding challenges to try:

- Make creepers appear 80% of the time instead of 50%.

- Make chickens rotate to a random angle when they appear.

- Make creepers move. (Hint: you'll need to add a ".creeper" section to your CSS file. Check the animation section for more help.)

- Make it so that Steve appears very rarely. He should be worth 100 points when clicked.

Don't worry if you can't meet these challenges right away! You'll have to really think about your code and the strategies we've learned, so take it slowly. If you remember to change or add just one thing at a time, you're bound to find the solutions sooner or later.

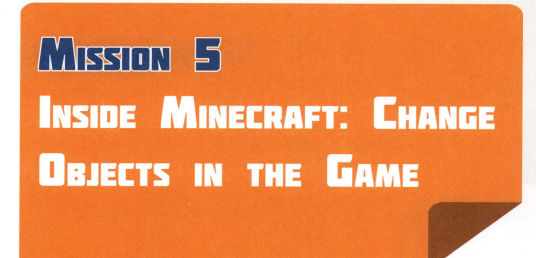

MISSION 5
INSIDE MINECRAFT: CHANGE OBJECTS IN THE GAME

You've made tweaks to the creeper game you built with your own coding. But you can also use coding to make changes to existing games. What have you always wanted to change within Minecraft? Let's start with changing the way objects look.

How would you paint the Minecraft world?
Try these secrets to bring mods to the game!

LET'S GET SET

1. The first step is to **GO BACK TO THE RESOURCE PACK** we created in the Making Music Mission 5 (page 74). Inside it, we created a folder called "sound", remember? In the same folder that has sound in it, create one called **"TEXTURES"**.

2. Inside the "textures" folder, **CREATE THREE MORE FOLDERS** called "blocks", "entity", and "items".

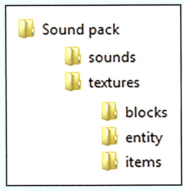

Whenever we want to replace a particular object's appearance, we put it in one of these folders.

- **THE BLOCKS FOLDER** is for standard blocks like dirt, sand, or grass.
- **THE ENTITY FOLDER** is for creatures like pigs, wolves, or skeletons.
- **THE ITEMS FOLDER** is for weapons, tools, and such.

3. We need to make sure we have the right file name when we add a new texture, though. Luckily, there's an easy way to find out what this is for any object in the game. Go back to the Minecraft home folder. On Windows, it's at:
C:\USERS\[YOUR_USERNAME HERE]\APPDATA\ROAMING\.MINECRAFT

On Mac, it's at:
~/LIBRARY/APPLICATION SUPPORT/MINECRAFT/

You'll see a folder called "versions". Enter it, and then click the folder for the version of Minecraft you have. There are two files inside, but the one we're interested in is the larger of the two. You can see which one this is by looking at the "size" section on the right.

IF YOU'RE USING A WINDOWS PC:
Click the View tab at the top of the page. You'll see a checkbox that says "File name extension". Click it.

View					
Extra large icons	Large icons	Medium icons		Group by ▾	☐ Item check boxes
Small icons	List	Details	Sort by ▾	Add columns ▾	☑ File name extensions
Tiles	Content			Size all columns to fit	☐ Hidden items
	Layout			Current view	Show/hide

IF YOU'RE USING A MAC:
Select the file and choose "Get info". Beside "Name and Extension", you'll see a little triangle. Click it. If the "Hide extension" box is checked, uncheck it.

Okay, now you should see that the file has ".jar" at the end. **RENAME THE FILE** so that it says ".zip" instead. Now, **OPEN THE FILE**.

GO INTO THE "ASSETS" FOLDER, THEN "MINECRAFT", THEN "TEXTURES". This is where the game keeps all of its default textures! You can go into the "blocks" folder to get the correct name for any blocks you'd like to change, "entity" folder for any creatures, and so on.

> grass_side_overlay.png
> grass_side_snowed.png
> grass_top.png
> gravel.png
> hardened_clay.png

READY TO GO!

4. We'll start with an easy one. **THE GRASS TEXTURE IS CALLED "GRASS_TOP.PNG".** You can click it and select "Extract" to save the file somewhere else, like your desktop. Try this now! Once you're ready, **OPEN THE FILE IN YOUR FAVORITE DRAWING PROGRAM**.

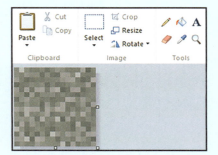

It's really small, isn't it? Zoom in a few times to make it a bit bigger. There's something else weird here: Grass is green, but it's showing up as gray in our program. That's because Minecraft files make parts of some blocks see-through, and some drawing programs can't handle it. Don't worry—this isn't going to be a problem.

5. Try changing how this file looks. You can **DO WHATEVER YOU LIKE—CHANGE THE COLOR, DELETE EVERYTHING AND DRAW YOUR OWN GRASS, ADD TEXT**, the list goes on. You can even make the image larger if that's easier for you. In the example below, I started from scratch and drew some new grass with some flowers.

The trick here is to draw something that won't look strange if it's repeated over and over. For instance, if you draw one big flower right in the middle, that will appear on every block of grass in the game. Sounds funny, right? Well, it would look a bit funny, too:

There's only one rule: The image has to have the **SAME HEIGHT AND WIDTH**, or it will display purple and black squares. This looks strange, especially for a block like grass, which are everywhere.

6. Once you're finished drawing your grass, **SAVE THE FILE AS "GRASS_TOP.PNG".** Move it into your resource pack, remembering to put it inside the "blocks" folder. Load up Minecraft and remember to select your resource pack from the Options menu if you disabled it earlier.

When the game loads, you should see that the top of the grass has changed!

Hey, there's a pig. Can we can change how he looks?

CAREFUL WITH MODDING   X

When it comes to modding Minecraft, lots of people like to download mods from the Internet. The problem is that if a mod doesn't work on your version of the game, Minecraft might not run properly anymore. If this happens, you have to delete the mod, which is sometimes easier said than done. To be safe, **always ask a parent's permission before installing any mods from the Internet**. Better yet, ask them if they can read about it and install it for you, since it's often a pretty tricky process.

5. The pig's texture file is stored inside the "entity" folder of the zip file we opened earlier. **COPY THIS FILE AND OPEN IT IN YOUR DRAWING PROGRAM.** Notice anything weird about it?

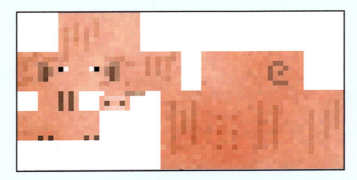

6. Everything in Minecraft is made out of boxes, so the **TEXTURE FILES ARE MADE UP OF PARTS** that the game can fold together to make an animal. Here, let's make it easier to understand:

The shape on the left is called a net. **NETS ARE 2D SHAPES THAT CAN BE FOLDED UP TO CREATE 3D SHAPES.** In this case, the net on the left creates the cube on the right. The net of the pig is exactly the same, just a bit more complicated. This means that if we draw a straight black line across the pig's net, you'd see several black marks on it in the game. So we have to think carefully about which parts of the net represent specific parts of the pig.

How do we know which parts of the pig are which? It can be difficult, but there are a few clues. We can see where the eyes, nose, and tail are, so why don't we start there? **TRY DRAWING A PAIR OF SUNGLASSES OVER THE EYES**, like so:

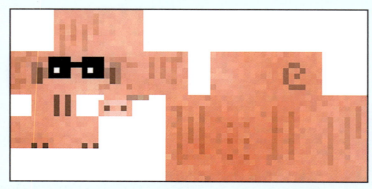

7. SAVE THE FILE AS "PIG.PNG". Inside your resource pack's "entity" folder, create a new folder called "pig" and put your drawing into it. Now, restart Minecraft and look for a pig. You could also spawn one using a pig egg in creative mode.

Excellent work! We've made those pigs *at least* 50% groovier.

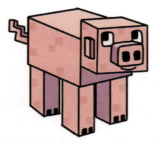

YOU CAN DO THAT?!   X

Play around for a while, and when you're ready, **why not take on the following challenges?**

- Make all the chickens blue.

- Write "Home Sweet Home" on the side of a block, and use it like a painting in your house.

- Make all the cows wear socks.

- Change the way a sword looks.

GLOSSARY

Don't know what a particular word means? I've made a list of all the words you might be confused about and explained them right here. Check it out, and impress your friends!

ARRAY: A special kind of variable that holds multiple values instead of just one.

ASSETS: Things like images and audio files that are used with your website or program.

CSS: Cascading Style Sheets. CSS files are used to change the way elements on an HTML page look or act.

ELEMENT: An item on a web page. An element can be anything: an image, a <div>, a table, even text.

FUNCTION: A collection of code that is grouped together so it can be run at a specific time, without having to retype it all.

HTML: HyperText Markup Language. This language is used to create the basic structure of a website.

JAVASCRIPT: A scripting language that is used to add extra features or functionality to a website.

JQUERY: A JavaScript plugin that can change the way users interact with elements on a web page.

LOOP: A way of running a section of code multiple times in a row without typing it all out each time.

MOD: Short for modifying or modification. To mod software means to change the way it works.

PARAMETER: A value that is given to a function to customize it or change its outcome.

PLUGIN: A package of code designed to improve existing software. These often add new features, or make it easier to do complicated things.

SCRATCH: A website that lets you build basic programs using blocks instead of typing code.

SETINTERVAL: A JavaScript function that lets you repeatedly run a section of code at a specific time.

SPRITE: A character image. In this book, Steve, creepers, chickens, and eggs all have sprites.

TAG: The building blocks used to build HTML websites. Tags are always surrounded with pointy brackets, and usually closed with another set and a forward slash in front of the first letter. For instance: <head> opens the tag and </head> closes it.

VARIABLE: A value that is given a name and stored to be used again later.

TROUBLESHOOTING

If your code isn't working properly, don't worry! Nobody makes programs that run perfectly the first time they try. In fact, facing problems will actually make you a better coder as you figure out where you went wrong. Below, I've listed some common coding problems and their solutions.

TEXT IS SHOWING UP ON MY WEB PAGE WHEN IT SHOULDN'T BE

Usually, this means you haven't closed an HTML tag properly. For instance, if you've typed <p> </> instead of <p></p>, your webpage will say "</>".

It could also be that you haven't closed your quotation marks properly. If you have quotation marks inside another set, it's important to use both single marks ('test') and double marks ("test") to help keep things easy to understand.

This would work:

```
$('#mainsection').append("<img class = 'egg'/>");
```

This would not:

```
$('#mainsection').append("<img class = "egg"/>");
```

In the second image, jQuery thinks we've tried to connect a string saying "<img class =" to the word "egg". Instead, "egg" should be in single quotation marks.

A JAVASCRIPT FUNCTION DOESN'T RUN

There are a lot of reasons why nothing happens when your function is supposed to run. However, most web browsers have an easy way to find out what the issue is. If you press the F12 key on your keyboard and click the Console tab that appears on the right-hand side, you'll see some red text explaining what the problem is.

```
⊗ Uncaught SyntaxError:          animation.html:59
  Unexpected token )
```

Here, it tells us that the problem is in the "animation.html" page, near line 59. Now, the problem is that we've forgotten to close a bracket, so we'll need to find the missing one and enter it in the right place.

Another common issue is typing a variable name incorrectly. In the case below, the variable is actually called *eggCount*, not *egCount*. Simply type the correct name and the code will run.

```
❌ ▶ Uncaught ReferenceError: egCount is not defined  animation.html:67
```

Here are a few things to do if you really can't find the problem:

- Make sure all of your functions and variables are typed correctly.
- If your jQuery isn't working, make sure you've added the links to the <head> section of your HTML page.
- Check your setInterval functions. If the repetition time is set too high, it might seem like nothing is happening.

YOUR CSS ISN'T WORKING

The most common reason for CSS not applying is forgetting to add the link to the top of your HTML page. It could also be that you've mistyped something, like "background-color" instead of "background-color".

If you've checked both of these things, make sure you're actually pointing to the right CSS file. The name of the CSS file should go into the "href" part of this code:

```
<link rel="stylesheet" type="text/css" href="style.css">
```

Having problems with a specific element? Remember that to select an object by its ID, you have to add a "#" in front. To select one based on its class, you add a dot (.):

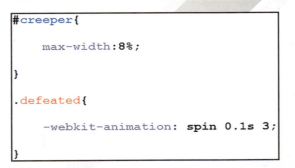

```
#creeper{

    max-width:8%;

}

.defeated{

    -webkit-animation: spin 0.1s 3;

}
```

IMAGES ARE TOO BIG, TOO SMALL, OR PARTLY OFF THE SCREEN

Computer monitors come in all shapes and sizes. All of the sizes given in this book are fine when viewed on a 24" screen at 1920x1080p resolution. That said, if you find that some things look strange, feel free to change their sizes in the CSS file. There's no problem with this at all! It won't change the way your code runs, although you may have to adjust the sizes of some other elements as well, particularly for the animation chapter.

ONLY SOME OF THE CODE WORKS

All of the code in this book was tested in Google Chrome (Version 65.0.3325.181). Unfortunately, not all web browsers have the same HTML5 compatibility, which means certain parts might not work correctly in other browsers.

If you're experiencing issues while using Google Chrome, turn off any pop-up blockers or ad-blocking extensions you might have. You can always reactivate these when you're finished working through the activities.

CODING
FOR
MINECRAFTERS

UNOFFICIAL ADVENTURES FOR KIDS LEARNING COMPUTER CODE

IAN GARLAND

Sky Pony Press
New York

Sky Pony Press books may be purchased in bulk at special discounts for sales promotion, corporate gifts, fund-raising, or educational purposes. Special editions can also be created to specifications. For details, contact the Special Sales Department, Sky Pony Press, 307 West 36th Street, 11th Floor, New York, NY 10018 or info@skyhorsepublishing.com.

Sky Pony® is a registered trademark of Skyhorse Publishing, Inc.®, a Delaware corporation.

Visit our website at www.skyponypress.com.

Authors, books, and more at SkyPonyPressBlog.com.

10 9 8 7 6 5 4 3 2 1

Cover art by Amanda Brack

Interior art by Amanda Brack and Ian Garland

Cover design by Brian Peterson
Book design by Joshua Barnaby

Print ISBN: 978-1-5107-4002-0
E-Book ISBN: 978-1-5107-4004-4

Printed in China